The World of Kew

Ronald King

The World of Kew

M

'It is impossible for any man to have Plants
to prosper, unless he love them'
[John Rea, 1665]

Endpapers: Map dated 1748 showing Richmond
Lodge and Garden and the buildings as they were
left by Queen Caroline. It also shows, in the right
hand lower section, the White House owned by
Prince Frederick of Wales and the grass fields
attached to it which afterwards became the
original botanic gardens.

Above: The Lady Fern, reproduced from *The
Ferns of Great Britain and Ireland* by Thomas
Moore and John Lindley, published in 1855.

Previous pages: A frosty morning on Pagoda
Lawn.

First published 1976,
Reprinted 1978 by
Macmillan London Limited,
London and Basingstoke.
Associated companies in Delhi, Dublin, Hong
Kong, Johannesburg, Lagos, Melbourne, New
York, Singapore and Tokyo.

British Library Cataloguing in Publication Data
King, Ronald, b.1914
   The world of Kew
   1. Royal Botanic Gardens – Kew
   I. Title
   580'.744'42195   QK73.G72R
   ISBN 0-333-24742-6 Pbk

Acknowledgments
The author and publishers are most grateful to
Professor John Heslop-Harrison, the Director of
the Royal Botanic Gardens, Kew, and to
Mr V. T. H. Parry, Chief Librarian and
Archivist of the Royal Botanic Gardens, for
permission to use the resources and facilities of
the Library of the Royal Botanic Gardens; to Mr
F. N. Hepper of the Royal Botanic Gardens for
the use of the Kew collection of transparencies;
and to those many other members of the Kew
staff who have assisted in ways too numerous to
mention. They would also like to acknowledge
with thanks David Warner Augustine Studios,
who was responsible for the design of the book
and Angelo Hornak for the special photography
required.

Printed in Hong Kong

Contents

Preface

This book begins with an account of the past of Kew but it would be wrong to infer from this a nostalgia for that past on the part of present-day Kew – modern Kew is very much 'with it'. The most up-to-date methods are in use in the culture and management of the living plants and new techniques are in the course of development. In its scientific work Kew is in the forefront of the particular branches of botanical science with which it is concerned and is involved internationally with many problems, including the pressing one of the conservation of endangered plants.

No more is said of these serious purposes than is necessary to present an accurate picture of the institution. The book has another aim – to create in the mind of the reader some of the love of plants and wonder at their beauty which pervades the works of the botanists and gardeners of earlier times, the feeling about plants which led John Rea to say, in the seventeenth century: 'It is impossible for any man to have Plants to prosper, unless he love them; for neither the goodness of the soil, nor the advantages of the situation will do it without the Master's affection.'

Let us now, therefore, join William Turner, England's first botanist, in his hunt for wild flowers through the woods of sixteenth-century Kew; listen to the Earl of Bute two hundred years later talking to Prince Frederick of Wales about some new plants for Kew from America; attend George III and Queen Charlotte in a walk into the botanic garden to see the delicate beauty of an orchid William Aiton has induced to flower; stand with Sir William Hooker in the 1840s watching the arches of the great Palm House arise from the earth; listen in to Sir Joseph, his son, as he discusses the implications of some botanical discovery with his friend Charles Darwin; and, in modern times, take a leisurely tour around the nostalgic seventeenth-century splendour of the Queen's Garden.

John Gerard, the Elizabethan gardener and apothecary, saw the earth as if it were 'apparelled with plants as with a robe of imbroidered works, set with Orient pearles and garnished with great diversity of rare and costly jewels'. Some of these 'imbroidered works' and 'Orient pearles' are set out in this book on display. If everyone saw the plant world through Gerard's eyes, there would be no need for anxiety about conservation. The spirit behind these words sustains those who work for Kew today and cultivate in the Gardens a 'great diversity of rare and costly jewels'. They do their utmost to maintain Kew as a haven of beauty, peace and serenity in a troubled world.

Ronald King
Weybridge, May 1975

The interior of the Tropical Fern House at Kew.

The Royal Garden

*'So sits enthroned in vegetable pride
Imperial Kew by Thames's glittering side.'*
Erasmus Darwin

If you had been in Kew in the year 1550 it is very likely that, sooner or later, you would have met, wandering about the country tracks, a stalwart man of about fifty years of age, dressed as a cleric, who seemed to be looking for something. Had you talked to him you would have recognised at once that he was a northcountryman. You would also have found out that he had two strong enthusiasms. He was a fervent supporter of the new reformed religion and he loved wild flowers: and it was for the latter that he was searching. Such a man was William Turner, who lived at Kew but served as chaplain to the Duke of

Left: Prince Frederick of Wales, from a print executed in 1753 by B. Baron after a painting by J. B. Vanloo. Frederick was one of the greatest royal art collectors and had a considerable interest in science. He also played cricket on Kew Green and became patron of Kent County Cricket Club.

Above: Page from William Turner's Herbal *with (tenth line from bottom) a reference to his garden at Kew.*

Opposite above: Eighteenth-century print of the White House, the Kew residence of Frederick, Prince of Wales, as modernised by William Kent. The building was pulled down by George III in 1802.

Opposite below: The lake at Kew as depicted in an eighteenth-century print. The Swan Boat was made in 1755 for George III's seventeenth birthday. It was named the Augusta *and its feet were 'artfully contrived as to supply the place of oars'.*

A View of the Palace at Kew. from the Lawn.

A View of the Palace from the North side of the Lake, the Green House, & the Temple of Arethusa, in the Royal Gardens at KEW.

London. Printed for Robert Sayer in Fleet Street, & carington Bowles in

Somerset, then the owner of Sion House across the Thames.

William Turner was the first Englishman to study plants methodically. He collected his observations into a *Herbal* which, published in 1568, has earned him the title of 'Father of English Botany'. He grew plants from other countries in his garden at Kew, and, although we do not know where it was and there is no connection with modern Kew, it is a strange chance that this first student of plants should have worked on the very land where later the national botanic garden was established.

At that time Kew Gardens was no more than a waste of scrubby woodland and water, but it had already seen colourful human activity. For several hundred years English kings and queens had had a country palace at Richmond, a mile or two upriver from Kew. Kew was part of the royal estate attached to the palace, and some of the courtiers had houses there. Monarch and nobles must have crossed Kew daily on their way to hunt, take their pleasure, or do business. Many times, too, their ornamented barges must have passed Kew in pageant on the Thames as they made their way upriver to Windsor or down

PLAN
of the Royal Manor of
RICHMOND.
otherwise
WEST SHEE.
in the County of Surry;
in GRANT to
HER MAJESTY.
Taken under the Direction of
PETER BURRELL ESQ:
His Majesty's Survr Genl
in 1771. by Thos Richardson in
York Street, Cavendish Square.

to London. Indeed, they often landed at Kew, where there had been a landing-place since ancient times. The name Kew is, in fact, derived from the old words 'caye' or 'keye' for 'quay' or 'wharf' and 'ho' for a 'spur of land'; the two were run together to form 'Cayo', as it was spelt in an old document of 1327, meaning the 'landing place on the spur of land'.

Of the monarchs who loved Richmond Palace, perhaps Edward III fared the worst. He died there in 1377 and was stripped stark naked by his rapacious servants and mistress as he lay dead – a miserable end to a reign which had lasted for fifty years. His successor, Richard II, also loved Richmond but demolished part of the palace in anguish when his beloved Queen, Anne of Bohemia, died there in 1394. Henry IV, Henry V and Edward IV all used the palace, and Henry VII enjoyed it so much that when the old house was burnt down in 1499 he rebuilt it grander style, providing it with an extensive garden – the first great pleasure garden to be made in England. It is another quirk of chance that the first such garden, even though not actually on the same land, should have been made on the same royal estate as the later Kew Gardens.

Henry VII's daughter Mary, sister of Henry VIII, Queen of France for a short time in 1514 and afterwards wife of Charles Brandon, Duke of Suffolk, had a house at Kew. So later did Queen Elizabeth's favourite, the Earl of Leicester. Elizabeth and Leicester must frequently have ridden together through the woods of Kew, startling the beasts in the undergrowth with their passage and scattering the water-fowl from the ponds and inlets, where herons and cormorants fished, as they still do from the Thames bank today.

Elizabeth died in Richmond Palace, standing for a long day propped up on cushions in a semi-coma with her finger in her mouth before giving way to increasing weakness. After her, James I's two sons, Henry, who died young, and Charles I, both used the palace. Then the heavy hand of Cromwell fell upon the monarchy: Richmond Palace came under the hammer in 1650, eventually falling into ruin, and the royal domain passed into private hands. One link still remains with those times, however – the old red-brick house now known as Kew Palace, which was not really a palace at all, but a country gentleman's mansion built in 1631 and one of those erected at Kew by gentry attracted to the court. In recent years the 'Queen's Garden' has been created around this house, bringing together garden designs, ornaments and plants of the seventeenth century when it was built.

The Stuarts went, to be succeeded by the Hanoverians, and a change came over Kew. The former royal land between Richmond and Kew became two private estates, one centred around a house called Richmond Lodge in the southern part near to Richmond and the other around a house later called the White House, which was at the northern end near Kew village. The Richmond Lodge estate, bought by George II in 1721, included the part of modern Kew Gardens next to the river, the White House estate – acquired by his son Frederick in 1730 -- the area away from the river.

George II's wife, Queen Caroline, loved Richmond and held her court there surrounded by her ladies, several of whom were noted beauties. Although the estate was used as a country retreat, Caroline had some pretensions to learning, and literary figures such as Alexander Pope, the poet, who lived at Twickenham, frequented the court. One of Caroline's enthusiasms was the Richmond Lodge estate itself. She got Charles Bridge-

Opposite above: John Stuart, Earl of Bute, who was held in great regard by Princess Augusta after her husband's death in 1751 and was a father-figure to the young George III, whose Prime Minister he eventually became. The appointment was not popular, however, and in 1763 Bute had to resign. The establishment of the botanic garden at Kew owed much to his enthusiasm for botany.

Opposite below: Burrell's map of the King's estates at Kew prepared in 1771.

Below: Kew Palace or Dutch House, the oldest building in Kew Gardens, was built in 1631 for Samuel Fortrey, a Dutch merchant, on the site of an older house which might have belonged to the Earl of Leicester, Queen Elizabeth's favourite.

Below: The Pagoda at Kew when it was first built. Each storey was finished with a projecting roof; round each storey was a gallery enclosed by a rail. The angles of the roof were adorned with dragons covered with coloured glass and furnished with bells.

Below centre: Princess Augusta of Saxe Gotha as painted by Jean-Etienne Liotard. Princess Augusta married Frederick when she was only seventeen. Her early married life was difficult because of the strained relations between her husband and his parents but, tactfully, she did nothing to make matters worse. She absorbed her husband's ideas, including his interest in exotic plants, and carried them on after his death.

man, a leading landscape gardener of the day, to lay out the garden. In using Bridgeman, Caroline was well up with the fashion, as he was one of the group of landscape gardeners who effected the transition from the formal gardens and clipped hedges of William III's time to the 'natural' style of the eighteenth century. Horace Walpole credits him with the invention of the 'haha' – the ditch and small fence which prevents access without impeding the view. He provided the Richmond Lodge garden with some ornamental buildings. Two of these, the 'Hermitage' and 'Merlin's Cave', both of which were within the boundary of modern Kew, were so extraordinary that they caused a considerable stir and much speculation as to what they represented.

Prince Frederick employed the architect and designer William Kent to modernise the White House. The garden was already famous, having been described by the diarist John Evelyn some fifty years before as containing 'the choicest fruit of any plantation in England'. Frederick met John Stuart, Earl of Bute, in 1747. Bute was a keen botanist and under his influence Frederick began to import plants from abroad and grow them in the garden of the White House. This modest beginning was in reality a great event for Kew, as it was the start of the royal plant collections.

The court at this time divided its time between hunting and other outdoor pastimes during the day and card-playing at night, but there were wonderful summer evenings when the strains of music floated over the water from the royal barges moored on the river while the fashionable crowd strolled and flirted on the terrace on the river bank. There can have been few among them untouched by the magic of those hours while the music played and the soft evening sky slowly darkened into a dusk pinpointed with a thousand lights from the boats rising and falling on the gentle Thames current.

These marvellous times were, unfortunately, too good to last. Frederick, in his enthusiasm for the garden, unwisely spent

Above: William Aiton, from a painting at Kew copied by E. Bristowe from a painting reputed to be by Zoffany. William Aiton had charge of the botanic garden at Kew from 1760 until he died in 1793. He must have had considerable skill as a cultivator, as many plants whose requirements are well known today were new in his time and methods of treatment had to be worked out from scanty prior knowledge. He was a kindly man – William Cobbett tells how Aiton took him in as a young lad and gave him a job.
Opposite above: The Orangery at Kew. In the days before fast fruit ships rich landowners built special glasshouses near or attached to their residences to grow oranges, which can stand outdoors in Great Britain in the summer only. The Orangery built by Sir William Chambers for Princess Augusta is a particularly elegant specimen of its kind and a fine example of the eighteenth-century classical revival in architecture.
Opposite below: Sir William Chambers. Chambers' appointment at Kew led on to a distinguished career as an official architect. One of his best-known works is Somerset House in London. He helped to found the Royal Academy in 1768. In 1770 he was made a knight of the polar star by the King of Sweden and George III allowed him the rank of an English knight.

too long a time in the cold one day in 1751 superintending the planting of some trees. When he got back to London, he fell asleep in front of an open window, and the resultant chill led to his death. His wife, Princess Augusta of Saxe-Gotha, was left with eight small children, the eldest being her son George. He was brought up in a very straight-laced way, his mother fearing that he would be contaminated by the fashionable vices. When he came of age in 1756 at the age of eighteen he was given a separate establishment in Kew Palace, on the other side of the road from the White House. On Bute's advice, Augusta appointed Sir William Chambers as her architectural adviser and tutor in architecture to the young prince. He was a wise choice. The influence of his *Treatise on Civil Architecture*, published in 1759, was as great overseas as it was in England and lasted long after his time.

Over the seven years between 1757 and 1763 Chambers embellished the Kew estate for Augusta with a number of buildings. He had been to China and was the principal exponent in England of oriental gardening, designing several Chinese buildings for the Gardens. The best known of these is the famous Pagoda, which was flanked with two other buildings, an Alhambra and a Mosque, which have not survived. Chambers brought his own special gifts of design to the classical style. He built the lovely Orangery, which is still one of the most elegant features of the Gardens, as well as a number of small temples, most of which have vanished, though three still stand today – the temples of Bellona, Aeolus and Arethusa. In order to carry a passageway for carriages and cattle over the main path on the eastern side of the gardens, Chambers designed a Roman triumphal arch, not as it might be when newly built but as the ruin that most Roman buildings had become, with fallen masonry and sculpture lying derelict

13

The White House at Kew was a royal family home from 1730 to 1802. George III was confined here during his period of mental disturbance in 1788. Fanny Burney the novelist, who was lady-in-waiting to Queen Charlotte at the time, accidentally met him when out walking with his attendants. Petrified at a possible 'fate worse than death at the hands of a mad king' she could think of nothing to do but run – and the King ran after her! When the attendants called her to stop, she turned in great trepidation and faced the King – to receive nothing more than a friendly kiss!

around it. This arch remains today almost as he left it.

In 1759 a gardener named William Aiton, who had been trained under the famous Philip Miller in the Chelsea Physick Garden, was brought to Kew as an assistant. In the following year Bute persuaded Augusta to set aside nine acres of ground near the White House as a garden for exotic plants and put this young man in charge of it, thus formally founding the botanic garden.

In this same year, 1760, young George was out riding when a message was brought to him that his grandfather, George II, had died. He returned home, and a few hours later a smart carriage with the blue and silver livery of the great William Pitt, Earl of Chatham, clattered over Kew Bridge and pulled up outside Kew Palace. The Prime Minister had come to tell George he was King.

Lord Bute was very unpopular and was thought by the mob to be carrying on a liaison with Princess Augusta. Every time there was a riot, and they were frequent, the crowd burnt a jackboot, symbolic of Bute, and a petticoat, symbolic of Princess Augusta, to show their feelings. Bute's influence soon waned, however, and George III brought in the famous landscape gardener 'Capability' Brown to sweep away all Queen Caroline's work in the garden of Richmond Lodge and turn that estate into a farm. The botanic garden flourished, and when Augusta died in 1772

Below: Page from the Kew Records Book of 1793, logging the plants brought to Kew by Captain Bligh in 1793 after he had successfully conveyed breadfruit plants from Tahiti (Otaheite) to the West Indies in H.M.S. Providence. Although the breadfruit plants were established successfully in the West Indies, it was not until emancipation, many years later, that the descendants of the slaves began to eat the fruit.
Opposite above: Eighteenth-century print of George III and Queen Charlotte walking in Kew Gardens.

Far left: *Sir Joseph Banks as a young man. Scientific work on the plants grown at Kew was in his lifetime done at Sir Joseph's house in Soho Square by botanists employed by him at his own expense as librarians. His interests extended further than botany, however. President of the Royal Society for many years, he had a finger in every scientific pie and in many others as well.*

Left: *Captain James Cook, who carried the young Sir Joseph Banks on his first voyage to the South Seas. Between them they named Botany Bay, afterwards the famous settlement. Cook also carried Francis Masson, Kew's first official plant collector, to South Africa on the first leg of his second voyage and was thus instrumental in fostering the early development of the Royal Botanic Gardens.*

15

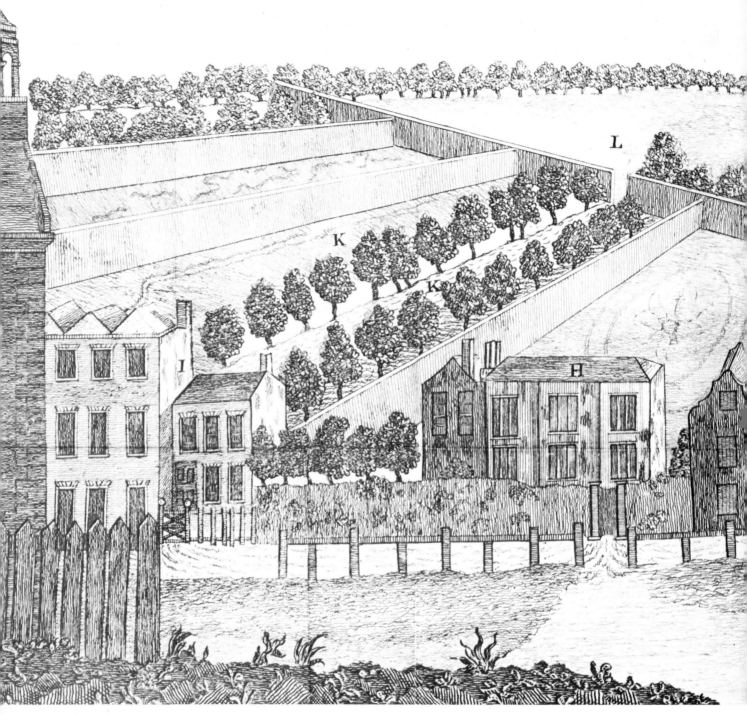

and George inherited the White House he not only kept it in being but gave charge of its direction to a remarkable man, Sir Joseph Banks, who had just returned with Captain Cook from his first voyage to the South Seas. On this journey they had explored some of Australia and it was doubtless Sir Joseph's description of the wonders of the vegetation of Botany Bay and other places they had seen which attracted George's interest. Richmond Lodge was pulled down and both estates began to be regarded as one, the title 'Kew Gardens' coming into use because the estate was formed from the two gardens.

For the next fifty years Banks kept up a massive correspondence with people all over the world who were likely to supply interesting plants for the King's garden. He persuaded George III to send out plant collectors, the first of whom was Francis Masson. One of the plants Masson sent back to Kew from South Africa in 1776 was a 'Kaffir Bread-Tree' which can still be seen in the Palm House at Kew. The collection grew so well that in 1789 William Aiton was able to list 5500 species that had grown at Kew in the *Hortus Kewensis* he published in 1789. The total had increased to 11,013 by 1814, when the

second edition was issued by his son William Townsend Aiton, who had succeeded to his father's post.

Among the plants listed were, of course, some that were to establish themselves as garden favourites. The first hydrangea, for example, was imported by Sir Joseph Banks in 1789. It began to flower while in the Custom House, the greenish tinge of its petals exciting considerable surprise and comment. From the Custom House it was taken to Banks's house in Soho Square for exhibition and then planted at Kew. In 1804 William Kerr, a Kew collector, sent home some plants from China in which he included the Tiger Lily. In the next few years W.T. Aiton grew many thousands of bulbs of this lovely plant and distributed them from Kew.

Banks was immensely interested in plants that could be useful to man, particularly those which, taken from their home country, were adaptable enough to thrive in another and add to the resources of their new home. One effort of this kind sponsored on behalf of the King was the voyage of the *Bounty* which, when the famous mutiny occurred, was in the process of

Above: Eighteenth-century political cartoon showing Kew Green. This picture was intended to show that Lord Bute and Princess Augusta were having an affair and that Bute could gain access to the White House where Augusta lived through a specially-provided back exit from his garden. The scene is of interest because it shows that the south side of Kew Green has changed little since George III's time and looked then very much as it does now.

Left: The Ruined Arch at Kew, one of the buildings designed by Sir William Chambers for Princess Augusta. It is a typical example of the kind of folly that eighteenth-century landowners had built on their estates in order to achieve a 'picturesque' effect. It remains today very much as Chambers left it.

transferring breadfruit plants from Tahiti to the West Indies as a source of cheap food for the slaves. Although Captain Bligh did not succeed in his task on this occasion, he did so four years later with another ship, the *Providence*, and as well as safely delivering the breadfruit he brought home to Kew a great many other plants.

For forty years Kew was the family home of George and Charlotte and their fifteen children who, as they grew bigger, were allocated various houses around Kew Green. The royal children and sometimes their parents could be seen driving or walking in Kew Gardens, which became a mecca for those who wished to see the royal family. Although they were narrow-minded, the royal pair set an example of the domestic virtues in an age when vice was admired. All through his life George had political troubles, from the Seven Years' War through the American secession to Napoleon. He also had to cope with porphyria, an unpleasant and little known disease which unbalanced his mind from time to time until, in the last ten years of his life, he slid down to permanent mental derangement. But there were many happy times before this, such as when he and Charlotte picnicked in the Queen's Cottage, studied botany (Charlotte was quite keen on it) or enjoyed a walk in the botanic garden to see something new which had come into flower.

While George III and Sir Joseph Banks were alive, the botanic garden continued to flourish. In 1815, indeed, two new

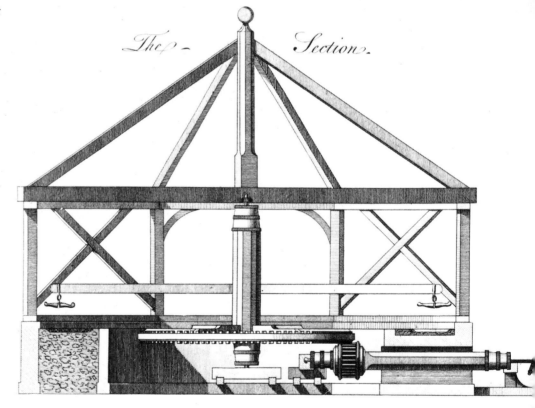

The — Section.

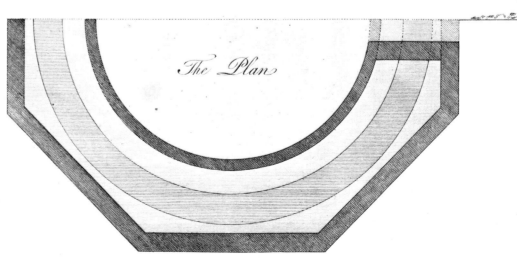

The Plan

collectors were sent out who added greatly to the collections. One of them, Allan Cunningham, won a place in history by his explorations of Australia and his discovery of the Darling Downs. In 1820, however, both George III and Banks died and the Gardens began to slide downhill. It was proposed to abandon them in the 1830s, but public opinion prevented this, and in 1838 a Committee of Parliament recommended that they be taken over by the state. Sir William Jackson Hooker was appointed Director in 1841 and a new era began. Under his rule, Banks's vision of a botanical garden serving as a repository of plant knowledge for a great Empire and directing the use of its plant resources to the best advantage began to come true.

In his first ten years Sir William greatly increased contacts with other institutions, nurserymen and individuals interested in plants. Although he was initially given charge of the few acres only which constituted the original botanic garden, he very soon came to control all the land of both the old estates. The southern half was leased away to form the Old Deer Park and the remainder landscaped by a noted designer of the time, W.A. Nesfield.

Many of the plants which came to Kew originated in warm climates. Those from tropical countries had to be grown in hothouses all the year round; others, less demanding, needed glasshouse shelter in the winter only. The palms, being mostly very large plants, were a particularly difficult problem. For them the great Palm House was built between the years 1844 and 1848. Other glasshouses were added and existing ones modified and extended to house particular families such as the orchids and cacti. The magnificent ironwork gates were also erected at this time, and many other improvements effected. By 1848, the Gardens had taken on the aspect they bear today.

In Sir Joseph Banks's time, Kew had confined itself to growing exotic plants, the work of classifying and naming them being done elsewhere. Hooker was a noted botanist, however, and though at first he carried on his scientific work in his own home, in the early 1850s his library and collection of dried specimens (a Herbarium) was established at Kew. This marks the beginning of scientific work at Kew. Other important collections were soon added, and within a few years Kew became a major botanical research centre attracting distinguished botanists from many countries. Towards the end of the decade Sir William received permission to embark on accounts of the plants of the Empire, and this work, modernised and updated in approach, continues today.

The garden itself attracted increasing attention from the public, and the number of visitors increased annually. On the advent of the omnibus and the railway it became easier to get to Kew, and a trip there became a great favourite with the poorer people of London's East End. From 1847 museums of plant products from the newly explored countries of the Empire were set up and proved a great attraction.

Side by side with this went the exploration and exploitation of the plant products of these countries. Men trained at Kew went out to the new countries to examine and collect plants, and though they often lost their lives very quickly from disease this did not deter others. They passed those plants which seemed promising back to Kew; these in turn were sent off to countries where they might be useful, to be tried out by other Kew-trained men. The great rubber industry of the Far East was founded in this way, and the widespread cultivation of the tree which produces quinine, the only specific against malaria until modern drugs were discovered, was also undertaken under Kew's auspices. There were many more such examples. Many countries owe a great debt, now rarely acknowledged, to those industrious men of Kew who gave their work and often their

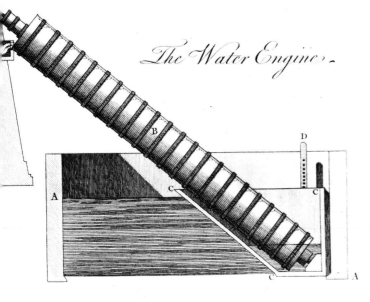

The Water Engine

lives to foster the trade which began their economic development.

Towards the end of his regime Sir William commenced another great project – the building of a glasshouse, larger than the Palm House, to accommodate large plants which, although nearly hardy, need protection in the winter. These plants are mainly natives of the warmer parts of the temperate zone and the house was therefore called the Temperate House. It consisted of a large central building with smaller ones attached. The whole complex was not completed until the 1890s.

Sir William Hooker died in 1865 and was succeeded by his son, Sir Joseph Hooker, a scientist of even greater stature. Sir Joseph was a close friend of Charles Darwin and provided him with much information useful to him in the development of his theory of evolution, standing by him in the stormy days that followed its announcement. He continued and expanded the work of his father and with money provided by Darwin began the compilation of the list of all botanical names which is one

Above left: The first girl gardeners at Kew. Their appointment caused a sensation. The Daily Telegraph *of 23 January 1896 reported that: 'A decided step towards the equalisation of the sexes has been taken by the Director of Kew Gardens, who, as an experiment, [has] engaged two young ladies as gardeners on condition that they wear trousers. Mrs Grundy, will no doubt, raise her hands in horror at the idea. . . .' The Director was permitted to recruit them only as boys, and they had to be dressed accordingly!*
Below left: The cover of a Victorian popular song about Kew showing a typical 'masher' (dandy) and his girl.

Above: Sir Joseph Hooker. As a young man Sir Joseph sailed with Captain Ross on the Erebus *and* Terror *expedition to the Antarctic. When he succeeded his father as Director of Kew he steadily pushed forward the policies his father had initiated. He did not have such an easy passage politically as his father and was involved in the 1870s in a long battle with the First Commissioner of Works about the extent of the latter's power to interfere with and control what was done in the Gardens.*
Opposite above: The interior of the great Palm House at Kew.

of the preoccupations of Kew and an essential tool for all botanists.

Almost from the time the botanic garden was founded, Kew has trained horticulturists for the highest posts in their profession, and in the 1870s this training was put on a formal basis. The modern course lasts three years, at the end of which the successful student is awarded the Kew Diploma.

As time has gone on the traditional work of plant classification has called into service evidence from plant anatomists, geneticists, biochemists and physiologists, and teams of scientists working in these fields as well as cell physiology now work at Kew. As Commonwealth countries have developed, the need for Kew's initiative in the economic area has greatly diminished, but although this work is reduced modern Kew has another reason for concerning itself with the dissemination of plants. Conservation of rare and threatened plants, and the role played in their preservation by botanic gardens, is now one of the most important subjects of study at Kew.

The more that is known about the plant kingdom by those whose daily lives are concerned with matters that affect the plant population of the world, the more chance there is that effective measures will be taken to protect what ought to be preserved. Gibbon said that, in the last resort, all taxes fall upon agriculture. A modern version would express much the same sentiment in a different way – all taxes fall, in the last resort, on the ability of green plants to capture energy from the sun and use it to produce food. The annual quantity of energy so captured in the great plant factories of the world like the tropical rain forests can be calculated mathematically. The rising population of the world is reducing its potential food supply by its ill-advised destruction of such factories for appar-

ent short-term gain which may eventually turn the land on which they stand into desert. The human species is thus in danger of emulating the Gadarene swine, which ran violently down a steep place into the sea!

Along with the destruction of the plants goes, of course, the loss of much that is worth retaining for reasons other than the loss of energy. Kew has sent plant collectors out into other countries to gather plants of value to man, and over the years many of these plants have been distributed from Kew throughout the world. This book records part of that story and describes in the following chapters some of the plant families and groups that, in one way or another, have specially interested the Royal Botanic Gardens. In the course of these chapters we shall climb the heights of the Himalayas and dive under the stagnant waters of lonely lakes; shiver in the cold forests of the north and swelter in the jungles of the tropics; suffer the pangs of thirst in the dry lands of the world and drink our fill of the heady drinks of the lands of the palm and agave. We shall be repelled by flowers carrying the rank smell of carrion and be ravished by the delicious fragrance of the sweetbriar leaf; be amazed by the giant bamboo growing visibly as we watch and equally astonished by the minute orchid a quarter of an inch high which hardly seems to grow at all. Above all, we shall see sights of immense majesty and beauty, from the rhododendrons, magnolias and camellias of the Asiatic mountainsides to the intricate tracery of a fern leaf; from the rainbow dazzle of the orchid to the browns and greys of the patterns of conifer bark; and from the noble sweep of great palm leaves to the grotesqueries of the cacti, which have no leaves at all. These, and a thousand things like them, are wonders to fire the imagination. He who is unmoved by them is to be pitied.

An Ancient Race

'Lo! Higher still the stately palm trees rise
. . . lifting their rich unfading diadems.'
Wilson: Isle of Palms

In the days of Rudolph Valentino, when the Arab sheikh was a figure of romance who carried the swooning heroine off to his secret lair, there to work his wicked will, the palm-tree of the desert shared in the story as he whispered sweet nothings to her in his private oasis. Nowadays, of course, the situation has changed, but the palm-tree retains the romance of old. Palms are denizens of the hotter places of the earth, and for those who live in the cooler regions they have always been a symbol of the exotic. The trees which they know best carry their branches and leaves all over them, like a mantle to cover their nakedness, but the palm-tree, in its commonest form, stands up gaunt and unclothed, bearing its giant leaves in a cluster at the top. Its

Above: *This dignified portrait is of Carl Friedrich Philipp von Martius. As soon as the Napoleonic wars were over, Maximilian Joseph, King of Bavaria, who had visited Brazil and been impressed by its vegetation, sent a natural history expedition to that country. Martius was the botanist selected to accompany it, and a better selection could not have been made. He produced, helped by the plant physiologist Hugo von Mohl and the palaeobotanist Franc Unger, three immense volumes of the* Historia Naturalis Palmarum. *The authors tried to elucidate every facet of the life of palms and set the outlines of the modern classification of palms. The work is the most magnificent treatment of palms which has so far appeared.*
Left: *The tall fan palms of the genus* Mauritia *are natives of South America.*

Opposite above: *A palm bearing leaves of the pinnate type, seen from below. Compare the leaf shape with that of the fan-leaved palm shown on page 26.*

Opposite right: *The central palm in this illustration, taken from the* Historia Naturalis Palmarum of *Martius, is the Coconut Palm, shown here with a native climbing to obtain the nuts while his family waits expectantly below. The Coconut Palm originated in Malaysia but is now widely distributed in tropical coastal regions, each tree producing from forty to a hundred nuts every year when mature, individual nuts being about 10 inches in diameter. The Attalea and Diplothemium palms on the right and left respectively are among the most ornamental of South American palms, the leaves of the latter being silvery underneath.*

very shape is alien to the dwellers in temperate lands and its romantic outline out of place in the landscapes to which they are accustomed. For them the palm-tree leans for ever over the waters of a Sahara oasis, casting a cool shade on the desert under the harsh African sun, or sheds its fruit on some far tropic strand where the sea is always blue. Yet the palm-tree has always held a fascination which could not be denied, and the great Palm House at Kew was built to satisfy the desire of our forbears to see these noble and immensely graceful plants at first hand.

Palms have been a part of human life since the earliest times. The Greeks and Romans used palm leaves as a symbol of victory – the winner was said to 'bear the palm' – and the Jews employed palm branches in their religious ceremonies. Solomon decorated the woodwork in his temple at Jerusalem with a palm-tree motif. The Christian church, adept at absorbing and transforming for its own use the customs of the pagans, marked the tombs and shrines of martyrs with palm leaves, signifying that they had come to victory through great tribulations. At the time of the Crusades, returning pilgrims acquired the name of 'palmers' because they brought home pieces of palm in honour of the occasion when they were carried on Christ's entry into Jerusalem. Indeed, the name Palmer lingers on as a common surname in our own time.

In tropical lands where palms are common they have been the means whereby primitive man has hoisted himself from

little above the level of a beast, without possessions or protection except his own body, on to a tolerable plane of reasonably organised, if not civilised, existence. The great Victorian naturalist, Alfred Russell Wallace, wrote a description of a South American village in which he showed how the life of the primitive community was built on the products of the palm-trees around them. Palms supplied rafters for the roofs of their huts and leaves to thatch them, split stems affording material for the door. They also provided a harpoon for catching fish and a stem and spines for blowpipe and arrows, fibres to make hammocks, bowstrings and fishing-lines, and spines for fish-hooks. A bassoon-like musical instrument was made from the stems. The Indian wrapped his precious feather ornaments in a cloth made from a palm spathe and made a crude chest for his other treasures from woven palm leaves. The ornamental comb on his head was made from palm bark. He made oil from one palm, ate the fruit of another and concocted a drink from a third. The mandioca pulp from which he made his bread was kept in a container fashioned from the bark of a climbing palm. Without the aid of the palms, his resources would indeed have been much reduced.

A similar account could have been written of almost every area where palms are found in quantity, and it is no accident that civilisation first arose in the country where the Date Palm abounded. The 'fertile crescent' of the Middle East where, the Greek historian Herodotus tells us, it grew in great numbers 'over the whole of the flat country' saw the first efforts of man to organise his life methodically. The palm provided him with many of his daily needs with so little effort that he had time to widen his activities beyond the mere struggle for existence. The importance of palms in the life of man cannot be over-estimated. Had they not existed, both pre-history and history would have taken a different course, and the slow climb of man from his origins to the present day would have been impeded.

Today, the products of the palm are still of immense importance. The Coconut Palm furnishes an immense variety of useful things. The kernel is used for food and its liquid contents, the 'milk', for drink; toddy can be made from the sap; the dried kernel, known as copra, yields oil and cattle feed; the husk, called coir, is used for brushes, saddles and upholstery. Other products made from various parts of the plant include mats, torches, combs, knitting needles, skewers, toothpicks, ridge poles, spear handles, shingles, hookahs, artificial boards and parts of musical instruments! This list is by no means complete, the Coconut Palm being probably the most useful tree known to man. The rattans of commerce are the stems of climbing palms, which have a host of uses as split cane for basketry, furniture and similar purposes. The Oil Palm is an important source of vegetable fat (so useful in margarine to those who wish to avoid cholesterol!); the Carnauba and other palms of wax; the Fishtail Palm of fibres, toddy and other products; the Sugar Palm of sugar, fibres, and toddy; the Sago Palm of sago, made from the pith; and the seeds of the Ivory-Nut Palm are used in making billiard balls and as a substitute for ivory in chessmen and inlays. The Betel Nut Palm provides the betel which, wrapped in a peppery leaf, with a touch of lime, is universally chewed in some parts of tropical Asia and the Pacific islands.

Young palms are grown and sold in quantity for the decoration of hotels and other meeting places – every hotel of any pretensions has its Palm Court! The Royal Palm and a number of others are planted in ornamental avenues in tropical countries and are also used for landscaping in other ways, although for this purpose palms are better planted individually, as their qualities are not favourable to massing. The Chusan Palm is hardy enough to be grown in temperate countries and is often planted, generally with a bizarre effect, since its appearance does not blend easily with other trees native to those countries.

Important though it has been for us, the relationship of the palm to man is an affair of the moment in the total life of the palm family – an incident of the last few minutes in a day that

dawned long ago. The palms are one of the oldest forms of
flowering plant and have maintained their primitive character
while other life has changed around them. They have been a
singularly successful family. Since they originated so long ago,
they have multiplied and diversified, so that there are now
several thousand species, spread across most of the tropical and
sub-tropical areas of the globe. There are said to be, in south-
west Brazil, solid stands of a single kind hundreds of square
miles in extent, the largest estimated to contain five hundred
million individual trees!

The leaves of palms are of two sorts. In some the leaf-axis
remains short so that the leaflets spread out like a fan, while in
others the axis lengthens so that the final form is like a feather.
The trunk gives the impression of being formed block by block,
the blocks being leaf-bases. As a new leaf is formed on the
crown, an old leaf is discarded. The old brown leaves hang for a
time and when they fall leave a stump, which in turn moulders
away and eventually falls or is knocked off.

Some palms adopt particular stem habits to meet local
circumstances. A few lift the stem off the ground on stilt roots
to keep it above flood level in their swampy habitat. Some grow
obliquely, such as the American Ivory-Nut Palm, becoming
prostrate towards the base. The Nipa Palm has a stout horizontal trunk which barely lifts its rosette of leaves above
the semi-liquid mud of estuaries. The stem of some South
American palms grows down into the ground as much as
eighteen inches before it turns upwards, thus protecting itself
against the worst effects of fire, for the stem reserves remain
unharmed if the top is burnt off. The Cuban Barrel Palm, as
well as some others, have swollen trunks, giving them the
grotesque appearance of a snake which has swallowed a meal.
Perhaps the most impressive are the wax palms which, ten to
twelve thousand feet up in the Andes, grow to a height of over
two hundred feet. Even these are dwarfed, however, by the
climbing rattan palm – a length of 556 feet has been recorded
for the stem of one of these. Another stem, longer still, was

To Her Royal Highness
The Princess of Wales
This Plate is humbly Inscrib'd
&c.

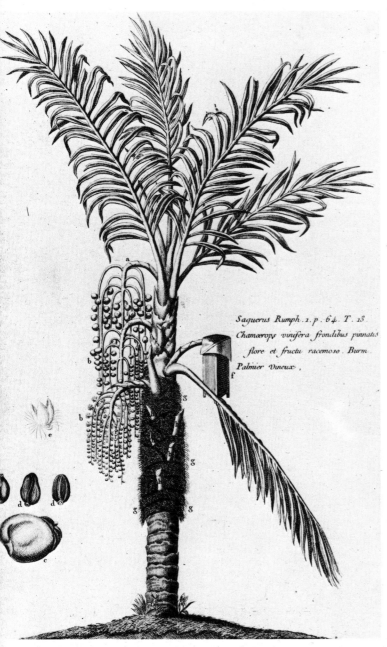

Saguerus Rumph.1.p.64.T.13
Chamaerops vinifera frondibus pinnatis flore et fructu racemoso. Burm
Palmier Vineux.

taken to be measured at the same time, but before it could be got out of the forest was unfortunately chewed up and trampled to bits by elephants!

Many palms are thornless, but others have thorny trunks, leaf-sheaths, stalks, leaflets, flowerheads and even fruits, the thorns and spikes being sometimes as much as a foot long. Some American kinds are so spiny that gloves have to be used to handle them. Palms provide a home for many forms of life. Their large leaves dictate to some extent the conditions which prevail around, on or under any particular tree, and these in turn dictate what other life will find the situation congenial. Fan-shaped leaves deflect the rain more than those of the feather type, and plants which find a lodging on palms with such leaves tend to be those which can stand drier conditions. If set with old leaf-bases, the trunks of those which let the rain through allow ferns, orchids, members of the fig family and small climbers to perch on them. The roots of these plants bind the old leaf-bases together, rubbish collects against the obstruction, and a refuge is formed where ants, beetles, spiders, centipedes, scorpions, lizards and frogs can find a home. Bees and wasps build in the drier parts, and climbing a rough palm can be a foolhardy venture! The Palmyra Palm is particularly hospitable – birds inhabit it during the night, while rats, squirrels, mongooses, monkeys and other small animals frequent it during the daytime.

In contrast with their giant leaves, individual palm flowers are small and unpretentious. Few are colourful, the finest in this respect being the Malayan Sealing-Wax Palm, which has scarlet leaf-sheaths and stalk and is very ornamental. Palm flowers achieve their effect by being massed in large, stout and often highly branched inflorescences. Some are very spectacular. The Talipot Palm sends up a flower-head twenty feet high with branches ten to fifteen feet long. As it does so the leaves drop off and the bare trunk stands like a seventy-foot pole carrying a head bearing the incredible number of up to sixty million green marble-like fruits. This palm requires forty to seventy years to reach this stage; it exhausts itself in this final massive outburst, thereafter becoming a rotting corpse slowly

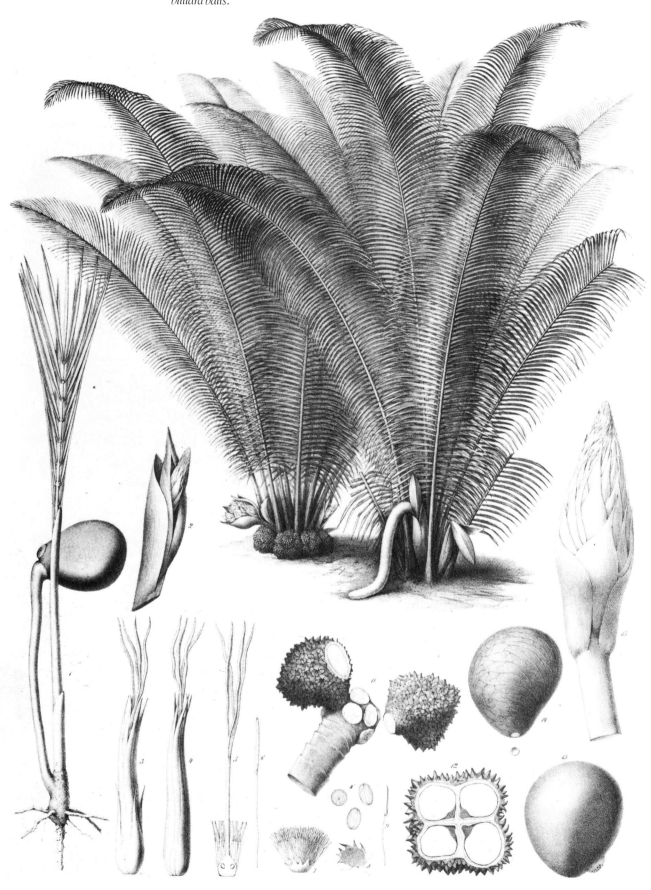

Engraving of the Ivory Nut Palm, taken from Florae Columbiae Specimina Selecta *published in Berlin by H. Karsten in 1859. The hard seeds of this palm are used as a substitute for ivory in chessmen and inlays etc. and for making billiard balls.*

Below: *The Date-Palm in flower.*
Bottom: *The Doum Palm, a native of north-east Africa and the only palm which branches naturally. The rind of its fruit resembles gingerbread, hence its second name of Gingerbread Tree.*
Right: *The European Fan Palm is the only palm native to Europe. It grows in abundance in the countries around the Mediterranean, reaching 20 feet.*

29

The first palms moved into the new Palm House at Kew in July 1848 were large specimens of the genus Sabal which may have been brought home by Captain Bligh in 1793. The roots, says a contemporary account, 'were enclosed in strong wooden boxes. To raise them to the surface of the ground the assistance of two engineers with tackle from Deptford Dockyard was obtained. One plant weighed 17 tons and the other not quite so much. They were . . . conveyed on rollers to the Palm House, a distance of nearly half a mile' from where they had been housed and were 'drawn up the steps of the east centre door by a windlass'.

Below: Engraving of a fan-leaved palm taken from Florae Columbiae Specimina Selecta *by Karsten, showing the elegance and beauty of form of these plants.*
Right: *A group of Palmyra Palms in Sri Lanka. This species is well adapted for sheltering animals, and hence it is resorted to by birds at night and by rats, squirrels, mongooses, monkeys and other small fauna during the daytime. The number of bats occupying it is sometimes so great as to be almost incredible.*
Below right: *Berthold Seemann, a German by birth, who came to Kew to train as a student-gardener in the 1840s and afterwards became a distinguished plant collector and botanist. Seemann wrote a book recounting his experience of palms in the wild.*

disintegrating until it finally collapses in debris.

Palm fruits are very various. All are fairly large and usually contain only one large seed. They have no mechanism to expel the ripe seed as is common in other plant families. The two palm fruits which are known to everyone, the coconut and the date, represent the extremes, the one being very large, hard and difficult to penetrate, the other comparatively small, soft, sweet and attractive. Most palm fruits develop a pulpy wall and are brightly coloured when ripe – yellow, pink, orange, red, purple or black. The cultivated date is by far the sweetest. The living things which enjoy palm fruits are legion, varying from the elephant which has a passion for the fruit of the Palmyra Palm – the largest succulent palm fruit, six to eight inches in diameter and containing three large seeds, each in a very hard stone – to the organisms which rot away the refuse.

The attraction of the fruit for living things is, of course, a most efficient way of ensuring that the seed contained in it is dispersed. Some palms rely on other means, however. A great many seeds are spread by floodwater in the swampy forests, and, indeed, the fruit of the Nipa Palm and the Coconut Palm are specially adapted for conveyance by water. The former lives on sandbanks of brackish tidal rivers and drops its hard nuts into the water where they float, slowly germinating, until they lodge in a habitat like that of their parent. The fruit of the latter also floats away, but as it does not tolerate salt water so easily it does not germinate while afloat but waits until it reaches a congenial situation.

Palms are difficult to study because many of them grow far from centres of learning and in remote and inaccessible places. They are also in the main very large plants which cannot easily be taken away from their habitat for examination. The collection of knowledge about them has therefore been relatively slow. Attemps were made in the eighteenth century to grow some in Great Britain, and six kinds were recorded as growing at Kew in 1768. These must have been small plants, as the small glasshouses of the time could not accommodate anything large. Their size, indeed, caused endless difficulty, because they continually outgrew whatever shelter was provided. It was realised that they could not be shown satisfactorily unless adequate height and space were provided for their tall trunks and wide spreading leaves, and eventually the Palm House was built – the first attempt to provide a building in which they could reach something like maturity.

The palms are second only to the grasses in their usefulness to man. While there are many more colourful families, few equal the palms in grace and beauty. Let us, therefore, enjoy to the full, wherever we may see them, these noble plants, which have been so successful in the struggle for survival and so useful to the human race.

Top: External view of the Palm House at Kew showing its graceful lines. The building was designed by Decimus Burton and constructed by Richard Turner, engineer, of Dublin. It is of great interest in the history of ironwork as it was built of wrought iron 'deck beam scantlings' at the same time as the first large iron steamships were being built and was, at the time, a novel application of the technique which made their construction possible.
Above: The fruits of a palm in the Palm House at Kew. Palm fruits are of great diversity, varying from the enormous double coconut of the Seychelles, which can weigh up to 50 lbs, to the soft sweetness of the much smaller date.

31

Beauty Herself

Long before there was anyone to appreciate its beauty, the wild rose was blowing in the woods and meadows, trailing down the banks in the summer sun and scenting the air with its glorious perfume. When man raised himself above the dust from which he was made, he saw the wild rose of the greenwood and straightaway fell in love with it. He brought it in to grow around his house, so that its loveliness and fragrance would be with him always. It is there still, constant and serene, ready to fill his heart with its sweetness, if he will only give it room.

Far back down the corridors of time, dwindled by distance as though viewed through the wrong end of a telescope, but bright and clear as a tiny cameo, can be seen the great King Sargon, dread ruler of Sumer and Akkad nearly five thousand years ago, leading his troops in a military foray over the Taurus. In the booty they brought back, solemnly recorded in the report upon stone which the great king caused to be drawn up, were coveted vines and fig trees – and also rose trees! Even in those far off days the beauty of the rose drew men like a magnet.

Out of the ashes of the kingdoms of Sargon's time and those that followed it arose the great empire of the Persians. Their wise men, the Magi, who were venerated far and wide for their knowledge, held the red rose in high regard. Red like the colour of fire, it attracted the fire worshippers of the twelfth century BC who cultivated it for their religious ceremonies and placed it under the special protection of an archangel.

The Greek historian Herodotus recorded many unlikely things in his *History* that were formerly thought to be fables but which, under the vigilant scrutiny of modern research, have turned out to be true. At the gardens of Midas in Phrygia, so he wrote, there grew a wonderful treasure – 'roses so sweet that no others could equal them, and their blossoms have as many as sixty petals apiece'. If this were thought a tall story by his contemporaries or those who came later, it is not so for us. With this reference, one of the great roses of the world may well have entered quietly into the pages of history, for it is very likely that Midas's rose was the Autumn Damask of modern times.

The Greek Theophrastus, who lived in the fourth century BC, a little later than Herodotus, carefully sorted out the plants he knew, distinguished one from another in his treatises on the *History of Plants* and the *Causes of Plants* and settled their names and relationships. In so doing, he noted that some roses had five petals, some twenty and some a hundred, and that the lucky inhabitants of Philippi in Thrace were able to collect the many petalled kind from the mountains of Pangaeus. He distinguished between this type, which he called a Rhodon, and those with a few petals, which he named the 'Dog' Rose. He knew that growing roses from seed took a long time and that more rapid results could be got by cuttings, and in his methodical way he set down for all time what was known about the rose and its culture in ancient Greece.

Even the down-to-earth Romans, whose minds turned ever towards practical things, were fascinated by the rose. In the first century AD they brought to Rome for their delight the red rose grown in Miletus, which they thought was of surpassing beauty and which Pliny said had twelve petals. The roses grown at Paestum, of which Virgil sings in his *Georgics*, flowered twice a year and thus can almost certainly be identified as the Autumn

The rose that grew over the grave of Omar Khayyam, the Persian poet and philosopher, at Naishapur was a Damask Rose. A seedling from it was planted in 1893 on the grave at Boulge, in Suffolk, of Edward Fitzgerald, who translated Omar's Rubaiyat into English. From this seedling many plants have been established elsewhere.

Opposite: Rosa moschata, the Wild Briar of the Himalayas.
Below: Rosa persica, found in Persia and Afghanistan, is rarely cultivated in British gardens and is hard to grow except under glass.
Bottom: Hybrid Tea 'Gail Borden', with large bi-coloured flowers.
Right: One of the China roses that carried the 'tea' scent, reproduced from Les Roses by P. J. Redouté, the most famous of all rose painters.

Damask Rose, which is the only one of the old varieties with this trait. Those to be seen in the long-buried frescoes of Pompeii were probably also the Autumn Damask. Such was the demand for roses in Italy that they were grown in Egypt for the Roman trade, and in Italy herself inventiveness was stimulated by the rewards to be gained from out of season blooms, hot houses heated with hot water being built in which roses could be forced in winter.

The wealthy Romans crowned themselves with roses at their banquets. Anything whispered quietly between guests was therefore *sub rosa* – a phrase still part of our language. In legend, Cupid gave a rose as a bribe to Harpocrates, the god of Silence, and for this reason a rose used to be suspended from the ceiling at meetings where secrecy was required, as a symbol and warning to those present not to reveal what was said. Is this the origin of the term 'ceiling rose' still used for light fittings?

The passion of the pagan Romans for the rose was hardly likely to endear it to the Christians, though, like so many other pagan things it became caught up in Christian practice: 'Mystical Rose: pray for us' sang the faithful in the Litany of the Blessed Virgin, and the rose continued to be cultivated throughout what used to be called the 'Dark Ages'. A dwarf red rose appears in the sixth-century *Codex Caesarius* at Constantinople, and the Moors in Spain cultivated a dark red rose in the twelfth century which tradition said had been brought from Persia five hundred years before. The love of roses had strengthened in Persia from age to age: the roses of Shiraz were famous, and the rosewater distilled from them was sent far afield. In the eleventh and twelfth centuries the great Persian philosopher and poet Omar Khayyam gave expression of the love of his nation for roses in his *Rubaiyat*, which celebrates the rose almost as much as it does the vine. A rose was planted over the poet's grave.

In the thirteenth century the land of France was filled with music. The singing troubadours, enthralled by beauty, could not lightly pass by such a lovely thing as a rose. King Thibaut IV of Navarre, Count also of Champagne and Brie, known as 'Le Chansonnier' and author of many songs, was away on a Crusade when he was struck by the strong but delicate perfume of a red rose growing in the war-torn gardens of the Arab lands. He was so attracted by it that when he returned home he brought the rose with him. It was grown at Provins, where it was discovered that, whatever was done with the flowers, the perfume persisted. The apothecaries of the town began to take advantage of this property by powdering up the dried petals and putting them in conserves and confections. These proved so popular that the practice developed into a substantial industry. The rose, in consequence, became known as the 'Apothecary's Rose', as well as the 'Provins Rose'. The 'rose from the land of the Saracens' enters into the famous French poetic legend *Le Roman de la Rose*, which was composed at this time.

Edmund Langley, Earl of Lancaster and son of the King of England, stayed at Provins in the thirteenth century and, in a fateful moment, chose the red rose of Provins as his emblem. So the Red Rose of Lancaster was born. In its typical form this rose has bright red semi-double flowers, flat when fully open and about four inches across. The White Rose of York is a rose which has been grown in gardens since ancient times. It was described by Albertus Magnus, the great thirteenth-century scholar who comprehended and wrote down all the knowledge

The Dog Rose, from Flora des Königreichs Hannover *by G. F. W. Meyer, published at Göttingen in 1842.*

The dog rose blooms in summer hour
On branches hanging low;
The light of heaven from each flower
Doth soft and sweetly glow

I take these blossoms to my heart,
That they may ne'er be blown,
And thus I do assure some part
Of heaven for my own.
Ronald King

Opposite far right: *A variety of* Rosa gallica, *the Provins Rose, depicted by Redouté, which had markedly bluish leaves. Rose growers have always sought interesting variations and many thousands* *have been put on the market over the years. As early as 1895, Kerner von Marilaun, a noted Austrian botanist, estimated that no less than 6400 had already been produced!*

of his time, as 'the white garden rose, which has often fifty or sixty petals'. This rose, he said, was 'very bushy', and its branches were 'long and thin'; the trunk 'often attains the thickness of one's arm'. The factions which bore the Red Rose and the White Rose as their emblems gave their names to the 'Wars of the Roses' of the fifteenth century. They fought each other over the pleasant land of England for many years, to the great detriment of the common people, until the ancient baronage was wiped out and a new dynasty ruled the land. The Tudor Rose, emblem of the newcomers and still the Royal Rose of England, is a heraldic combination of the York and Lancaster roses.

This heraldic rose has its counterpart in the garden. One of the Summer Damask Roses, a rose with a white background blotched with pink, has for long been called the 'York and Lancaster Rose'. Often confused with it, but easily distinguishable if both roses are seen together, is a sport of the Provins Rose known as 'Rosa Mundi', a pale pink rose heavily blotched and striated with red. In older writers the name of this rose is given as 'Rosamonde', reinforcing the tradition that its early history was bound up with that of Henry II's tragic mistress, the 'Fair Rosamond'. Its cultivation long ago suggests that it, too, might be one of the things we owe to the returning Crusaders.

The cultivated roses of those times were not the neatly pruned low-growing bushes or standards so familar to us today. Many of the wild roses are climbing or trailing shrubs with fierce prickles or thorns and are not infrequently rampant in growth, and the varieties that were bred from them in earlier times retained these characteristics. Botanists argue among themselves about the number of species of roses, and a cruel critic tells a story of a botanist who distinguished so many that the characteristics of two supposedly different were found on the same bush! The number varies according to the criteria taken, but there are certainly more than a hundred and probably more than two hundred. It is surprising, therefore, to find that modern research attributes the ancestry of all the roses except one that were in cultivation in the western world before

Above: Rosa gigantea *is the wild Tea Rose of China and one of the China roses that found their way to Europe to become the ancestors of modern hybrid roses. It is a rampant climber reaching 40 feet or more.*

1800 to four species only. Opinion based on genetic research is that these cultivated roses, the Provins Rose, the Damask Roses, the White Rose of York, the Cabbage or Provence Rose, the Moss Rose and some others, together with the hundreds of varieties which had been developed from them in the course of the eighteenth century and were in cultivation as that century ended, were the product, in various combinations and recombinations, of the hybridisation, often very far back and in the wild, of the old Red Rose (the Provins Rose itself), the Phoenician Rose, the Musk Rose and the Dog Rose. The exception was a large double yellow called the Sulphur Rose, the only yellow rose in cultivation before 1800, which was itself a species but did not flourish very well in the northern countries, opening its flowers fully only in hot weather: it does not seem to have entered into breeding.

The basic species from which the ancient garden roses were evolved differ quite markedly from one another. The Provins Rose varies in characteristics from plant to plant but is not one of the most vigorous, being in its wild form a small shrub three to four feet high with single deep pink to crimson flowers. The Phoenician Rose is a climber with white flowers; the Musk Rose is a tall-growing shrub of the Himalayas which bears single white flowers; the Dog Rose, which will be familiar to many readers as a common plant of the hedgerows, grows six to eight feet high and throws out long arching branches bearing pink single flowers; and the Sulphur Rose is a small shrub often barely reaching three feet in height. Not, one would have thought, a group likely to form the basis of our glorious modern roses, and, in truth, an infusion of new blood was needed before progress could be made.

The problem facing rose-breeders at the end of the eighteenth century was that of lengthening the flowering period of

Above: Rosa gallica *from a rare book,* A Collection of Roses, *published by Miss Lawrance in 1799. The rose depicted is the Provins Rose, the old red rose known to man from ancient times.*
Far left: Rosa centifolia, *by Redouté. Formerly thought to be ancient, it is now known to be of recent origin.*
Left: The fragrant-leaved 'Double Mossy Sweet Briar', by Miss Lawrance.
Opposite: The Sulphur Rose, by Redouté.

the garden rose. The new varieties which had been developed during that century were many of them most attractive, but, like their parents, they still flowered for a short period in the summer only, and their beauty passed all too soon. The Autumn Damasks threw a few flowers in the autumn but these were the sole exception. Then, quite dramatically, came the break. Four different kinds of China Rose, which had been grown for many generations in Chinese gardens, were imported and crossed with existing strains. These roses had been developed from two indigenous Chinese species, one a low growing bush and the other a tall shrub with long trailing branches. All four carried, in their genetic make-up, the factor of continuous flowering and so, as soon as these China roses were bred with existing varieties, that factor was passed on to the progeny. Two of them were 'tea-scented'.

New groups, the Noisette Roses and the Bourbon Roses, were produced almost immediately from these introductions.

The Noisettes were bred in South Carolina by a Charleston nurseryman, Philippe Noisette, between 1802 and 1840. They were climbing 'tea-scented' roses, a name which became shortened to Tea Roses. The Bourbon roses were bred about the same time from an accidental hybridisation that occurred in the island of Réunion off Mauritius, formerly called the Ile de Bourbon. This hybrid had semi-double flowers scented like the Autumn Damask which was one of its parents and flowered well on into the autumn. From this original Bourbon Rose many others were bred by crossing and recrossing. One is still grown today – the white thornless rose 'Zephyrine Drouhin'.

Further hybridisation in these groups gave rise to a number of beautiful roses which were widely grown between 1840 and 1890. Although the new Tea Roses were dwarf (that is, they did not throw long rambling shoots as did most of the wild species or old garden roses) and had a very long flowering period, they were not very hardy in northern Europe, still growing extremely well, however, in the southern USA and flourishing in the south of France.

Another group also developed which included the old red Rose of Provins, the Autumn Damask and Bourbon Roses in its pedigree, as well as one of the China Roses. This strain came to be called the Hybrid Perpetuals. In spite of its name this motley group flowered mostly in summer, throwing a few flowers only later. The Hybrid Perpetuals were, however, hardier than the Tea Roses and so kept their place alongside them in public esteem until 1890.

Rosa canina bourboniana *from Redouté's* Les Roses. *The rose Redouté has depicted under this title is the original Bourbon Rose that resulted from an accidental hybridisation that happened in the island of Réunion. It was the first of the Bourbon roses which were in vogue for a few years in the early part of the nineteenth century. These were used very extensively in breeding and played a considerable part in the early developments which led to the hybrids that furnish our rose gardens so beautifully today.*

Roses have another attraction as well as their beautiful and striking flowers. Many of them have brightly-coloured and attractively-shaped fruits. Frank Kingdon-Ward, the plant collector, described them in *Berried Treasure* as follows: 'The torrid vermilion urn-shaped hips of the Himalayan Rosa macrophylla, of the Chinese R. moyesii, and particularly of R. setipoda, set a new standard in winter colour. The hips of the last named, for example, reach a length of two inches and a half!

By reason of their size and weight, the loose bunches swing and loll on their stalks, arching them, and this careless grace adds to the beauty of the bush. So placed that the slanting sun strikes them full, the ripe hips of R. setipoda glow with a fierce unearthly light.'

A French rose-breeder named Guillot succeeded in 1867 in raising a cross between a Hybrid Perpetual and a Tea Rose, although he himself was uncertain as to its parentage! This rose, named 'La France', had the general habit of a Hybrid Perpetual but possessed also the fine-shaped buds and free-flowering characteristic of the Tea Roses. This was the first of the Hybrid Tea Roses, the group which has for so long held the stage in recent times. It was not until about 1890 that the new group came to the forefront, for the early crosses set very little seed, but as soon as this difficulty was surmounted they displaced both the Perpetuals and the Teas, their longer flowering season making them preferable to the former, their greater hardiness to the latter.

When they first became popular, the Hybrid Teas did not contain any good yellow roses. In the 1890s another French breeder, Pernet-Ducher, used another species, the Austrian Briar, to breed a rose he called 'Soleil d'Or', in colour a rich orange splashed with red. This was a poor rose in itself, but it was a rose with a destiny. From it were raised roses which brought into the Hybrid Tea range all the yellow, orange and flame colours so conspicuous in modern rose gardens. All stem from that poor hybrid of seventy years ago! At various times other species have been used: the Memorial Rose, a prostrate rose from east Asia with clusters of large single white flowers, produced the glossy-leaved 'Wichuriana' ramblers, and the Scotch Rose, a low, very prickly bush with white, pink or yellow flowers, led to other very attractive varieties.

Parallel with the development of the Hybrid Teas, the Japanese Multiflora rose, a strong climbing species with single white flowers, was used for breeding. From this was produced a group of perpetual-flowering roses, the dwarf Polyanthas, excellent garden plants because of the showiness of their large flower clusters, their great hardiness and their long flowering period. The Danish breeder Poulsen used Hybrid Teas to breed from these the Hybrid Polyantha group. Other breeders have

39

Above: Rosa noisettiana, *by Redouté, is the rose bred by Philippe Noisette of Charleston which gave rise to the race of Noisette Roses, the first roses grown in western gardens to carry the gene derived from the China roses which ensured continuous flowering from June until the onset of winter frosts.*
Right: *Redouté gave the title of* Rosa eglanteria *to this beautiful yellow rose, indicating that in his day it was regarded as a variety of the eglantine or sweet briar.*

40

41

'Among all flowers of the world the flower of the rose is chief and beareth the prize', wrote Bartholomaeus Anglicus in about the middle of the thirteenth century. Echoing him, the great naturalist W. H. Hudson said in Hampshire Days: 'Of all the hedge flowers, the rose alone is looked at, its glory being so great as to make all other blooms seem nothing. . . . Look at it here, in the brilliant sunlight and the hot wind, waving to the wind on its long thorny sprays all over the vast disordered hedges; here are rosy masses, there starring the rough green tangle with its rosy stars – a rose-coloured cloud on the earth and summer's bridal veil – and you will refuse to believe . . . that anywhere on earth, in any hot or temperate climate, there exists a more divinely beautiful sight.'

Above: *Engraving of the tea plant,* Camellia sinensis, *taken from* China Illustrata *by the Jesuit Athanasius Kircher, published in Amsterdam in 1667. The tea plant is, like its ornamental relatives, an evergreen shrub which grows naturally to a height of 15 to 30 feet, though in cultivation it is kept down, as shown in the engraving, to a height of 3 to 5 feet. In its general appearance it resembles the myrtle, the flowers being white, with yellow stamens. In the text accompanying the engraving the plant is referred to as* Cha, *the original Chinese name from which the western name 'tea' is derived.*

introduced strains of great colour and vigour, and the name 'Floribunda' has been adopted to express the free-flowering nature and brilliance of the flowers of the new roses. The modern bedding rose is far removed from the ancient garden roses and original species from which it was bred!

The development of the bedding rose as a compact plant suitable for formal displays in large gardens and public places and for small town gardens has, in fact, tended to obscure the virtues of the older cultivated varieties and the roses of the wild. Of late years, however, there has been a revival of interest in these roses, although they are still the taste of a connoisseur rather than the general run of gardeners. This is chiefly a result of the trailing or arching growth of many of them, which requires rather more space than gardeners are prepared to make available and renders them difficult to keep under control. A number of the wild roses have brightly coloured and decorative fruits called 'hips' which remain on the plant much longer than the flowers and lengthen the season during which they are an asset to the garden display. Given the amount of space they need and the support of a tree or wall when they require it, the old roses and the wild species can create a most graceful and attractive garden scene. When, in the falling dusk, the long curving sprays of the lighter-coloured kinds, dotted with flowers, catch the horizontal sunset rays, it is as if the garden were illuminated with rows of glowing fairy lights strung across it. As the red of the sunset deepens the darker shades come into their own, reflecting back the warm glow which is matched in their own colour.

Beautiful as roses are, they do not flower until the beginning of summer and cease when the cold days come. Until recent times, no flower in common cultivation at all resembling the rose did anything to fill the gap. In this century, however, the true virtues of a plant long known to the Chinese, and for two centuries to the western world, have at last been realised. The camellia, in Victorian times, was a flower of the wealthy, and, although much grown and appreciated in upper-class circles, was not known, as was the rose, by the average gardener, who thought it something exotic and out of his reach. The truth is, of course, that the camellia is a very hardy and tolerant evergreen shrub of easy culture, with the great virtue that it

Opposite above: *Tea Gardens at Rambada Pass in Sri Lanka. Tea is now grown in many countries where the climate is suitable. It grows well in monsoon lands from sea level up to 6000 feet but prefers the higher altitudes. The terrain shown is typical of tea country and is ideal for it. In general, commercial tea gardens are found in a belt confined to mountains near the equator within latitude 42 degrees north and 33 degrees south.*
Opposite: *A white variety of* Camellia japonica *reproduced from an illustration in* Illustrations and descriptions of the plants which comprise the natural order Camelliae and of the varieties of Camellia japonica cultivated in the gardens of Great Britain, *published in London in 1831. The book, one of the first of its kind in English, was beautifully illustrated by Alfred Chandler, the text being by W. B. Booth.*

42

begins to bear its flowers before the winter is over and carries a load of blossom through the spring when most other plants are little more than bare branches just beginning to stir into life. Not only that, even though it is not scented, its flowers bear comparison, for delicacy and beauty, with the finest roses. It is also thornless and of neater habit than the rose.

The home of the camellia is eastern Asia, where it is a common woodland plant, growing on rugged hillsides, in thin forest and down the sides of river valleys. It grows on the mainland of India, along the south coast of China and Japan and on the coastal islands of those countries. In favourable conditions it will make a tree with a trunk a foot in diameter and thirty feet high. Such a tree in full bloom rivals its fellows, the rhododendrons and magnolias, which are natives of the same region, in beauty and magnificence. Most of the garden camellias are varieties of the wild *Camellia japonica*, but *Camellia reticulata* and *Camellia sasanqua* and varieties developed from them are also grown. Botanically, the plant from which tea is obtained is a camellia, so that the ornamental plants have a relative of conspicuous usefulness!

Camellias at present cost more to buy than do roses, but, on the other hand, they live a very long time, growing larger and bearing more flowers every season, so that there is, in the end, a greater return for the money. The virtues of the camellia are such that it deserves to be looked upon as the complement of the rose, as essential to the garden at one time of the year as the rose is at the other, and no more difficult to grow. The rose has been a favourite flower in history, the symbol of elegance and perfection, associated always with romance and love. The camellia cannot show such an impressive impact upon man, although it, too, has had its moments – in the younger Dumas' *La Dame aux Camellias*, from which came the play *Camille*, and in Verdi's opera *La Traviata*. It may well be that its hour is still to come!

43

Top: Camellia reticulata, taken from Chandler and Booth. The flower illustrated was a cultivated form imported from China, the original wild species not being discovered until 1924.
Above: Camellia granthamiana *flowering in the Temperate House at Kew for the first time, on 3 November 1959. This new species was discovered in Hong Kong in the 1950s. Only one plant is known in the wild.*
Above right: *A variety of* Camellia x williamsii. *This group of cultivated camellias has been produced by hybridising* C. japonica *with* C. saluensis.
Right: Camellia japonica, *from which many beautiful varieties have been developed, as illustrated in Chandler and Booth.*

44

A magnificent cluster of camellias taken from a large folio work entitled A monograph on the genus Camellia, *which was published by Samuel Curtis in London in 1819. The beautiful drawings in it were the work of Clara Maria Pope.*

Secret Marriage

'We have the receipt of fern-seed, we walk invisible.'
William Shakespeare

In those faraway times when the coal measures that now form one of our most useful sources of power were laid down, one plant group, the ferns, flourished so well and left so much in the way of fossil remains that it must have been very abundant. From the evidence of these remains it is clear that ferns formed a very substantial part of the vegetation of those times; many of them were large trees which thrust their great leaves upwards towards the sky so that the chlorophyll in them (the substance that gives all green plants their colour) could catch and use the sunlight to make the food by which they grew. When we burn the coal we release that energy. The heat, therefore, that warms our legs as we sit by the fire and the electric light by which you may be reading these words is buried sunlight captured and held by the fern group more than 250 million years ago.

Ferns are, indeed, a good deal older than this, having their origins in very early ages a hundred million years before the coal was formed. The most ancient families have long ago died out. A living representative of one of the older surviving families is the Royal or 'Flowering' Fern. In spite of its secondary title, which is given only because of a chance resemblance, ferns are not flowering plants. They evolved long before flowering plants came on the scene and bear neither flowers nor seeds. Their world was predominantly a green one patched with shades of brown and red. The colour of flowers was still to come. There was no less beauty then than there is now, but it was beauty of form rather than of colour.

Although the ferns have no flowers, they have some characteristics of the more complex plants which evolved later. Their roots are true roots like those of more advanced plants and their leaves are true leaves. They also have specialised tissue in their roots and stems for the transport of water and plant food. They do not possess, however, one important feature which developed in the higher plants. There is no growing layer between the transporting tissue and the outside skin, so they cannot, in the way that more advanced plants do, add a ring of new supporting tissue year by year by the outward growth of this layer. Thus, although their stems may grow tall, they remain slender and lack strength. In the tree ferns this is partly overcome by the thickening of the outer layer of the stem and partly by a covering of roots which grows from the base of the leaves. The lack of this growing layer has undoubtedly been a handicap in the evolutionary struggle.

If they have no flowers, how do ferns reproduce themselves, for without flowers they cannot produce seed? The answer to this question was for a long time a puzzle to the early investigators, and for this reason they classed ferns as 'cryptogams', which means 'hidden marriage'. There is, however, nothing

Some of the illustrations of ferns used in this chapter are taken from The Ferns of Great Britain and Ireland *by Thomas Moore and John Lindley, printed by Bradbury and Evans in 1857. The originals were produced by a remarkable process, known as 'nature printing', first used in the Imperial Printing Office at Vienna, in which the plant itself was induced to make an impression on copper from which reproductions could be made. The illustration, being prepared from the actual plant, reproduced very faithfully the external characteristics of the surface, hairs, veins and other significant features.*

Opposite above: *Sir William Jackson Hooker, from a portrait by Thomas Phillips, R.A. Sir William's vision and imagination created the Kew that we know today. Commonwealth countries and some others owe much to his efforts to encourage the spread of useful plants and to foster trade in plant products. They also owe much to the beginning he caused to be made in the description and classification of their native plants. He devoted much time to the study of ferns.*
Left: *Illustration from the extensive collection of drawings by Indian artists (more than two thousand) made for William Roxburgh of the Calcutta Botanic Garden in the early years of the nineteenth century. The collection is at Kew.*

more hidden about the sexual processes of ferns than there is about those of flowering plants.

Ferns bear spores in containers on the backs of their leaves, often under protective scales. These have been sometimes removed by those who do not know their life-history, under the impression that they are the pest known as the 'scale insect'! Spores may be produced on all leaves or on some only. On the leaves which bear spores, they may be limited to certain leaflets, others being sterile. They are very tiny and dust-like, the number of spores produced by one frond amounting to millions. Where ferns grow the air is full of spores, which are capable of surviving for very long periods.

Although the specks of life which are the fern spores might be mistaken for seeds by those unaware of their true function, they are not seeds and do not develop into plants like the one from which they originated. When a spore falls on to a suitable surface of moist soil it begins to grow, forming a plant totally different in structure from the fern. Technically, it is organised like a very simple moss. The new plant is a thin, green, ribbon- or heart-shaped structure which lies flat on the soil like a scale. It is quite small, being less than half an inch wide. If you care to look, specimens may easily be found. A search around patches of fern in the autumn, particularly in such places as the moist bank of a hedge, should soon reveal some. Alternatively, some of the surface soil from such a location, placed under a tumbler and kept moist and close, will almost certainly produce a crop.

The new plant contains chlorophyll and thus is able to make

The invention in the 1820s of the Wardian case (in essence, a small portable greenhouse) enabled a far larger number of plants sent by sea to arrive alive than had hitherto survived. The Victorians were quick to see another use and adapted the idea, forming ornamental 'fern cases' to decorate their rooms. This sparked off a craze for fern cultivation and wild ferns were ruthlessly sought out and dug up, almost to the point of extinction, to meet the demand.

Opposite top left: *Tree ferns in Brazil. The nobility and grace of tree ferns has impressed many observers. They have been said to 'spread their fronds as wide as the state umbrellas of Asiatic Kings' and to 'exhibit the utmost development of tropical luxuriance and beauty'. They are particularly beautiful when seen from above. 'The view of their feathery crowns, in varied positions above and below the eye', said Alfred Russell Wallace in* The Malay Archipelago, *'offers a spectacle of picturesque beauty never to be forgotten.'*
Opposite: *A frond of the 'Lady Fern' from Moore and Lindley. The leaf-shape of this beautiful fern is very variable, drawing the comment from the authors that the 'forms in which the Lady Fern masquerades are remarkable for their elegance and valuable on account of the variety they afford as cultivated plants.'*
Left: *The Spleenwort or Wall Rue is one of the most common ferns in the northern hemisphere. The fern shown under this name in this elegant illustration from Moore and Lindley is a form which resembles the Maidenhair Fern and for this reason was called the Maidenhair Spleenwort.*

food for itself. Hairlike cells on the lower surface draw water and minerals from the soil, but the plant has no true root, stem or leaf. Two specialised organs develop on the underside. One produces tiny male cells each with whiplike hairs which enables it to move through the moisture. The other produces the female cell,. a single egg; and the male cells swim towards it, one eventually fusing with the egg. The fertilised egg begins to grow, living for a time on the host which produced it, but as it develops into a fern, the scale-like parent dies away, leaving the fern plant to mature and begin the process once again.

Reproduction in ferns is not confined to the sexual method. In one fern the leaves arch over and touch the ground at the tip, and when they do so, a new plant is produced at the point of contact. Thus the fern spreads by a series of steps and for this reason has been named the 'Walking' Fern. Since its progress is by no means organised, one plant can very soon form a very tangled colony! Another type produces small bodies on its leaves which contain food stored in two fleshy leaves. When detached from the parent these bodies are capable of developing into a new fern plant. As these small bodies behave in a way like bulbs, this fern has acquired the name of the 'Bulb Fern' Another, the Boston Fern. resembles the familiar strawberry plant in throwing out runners which are able to root and form new plants, a faculty that is common to many other members of the group.

Ferns are found. everywhere from the Arctic to the tropics, occurring in the greatest numbers in the tropical rain-forests. They particularly love the branches of the great trees of these forests and may populate individual trees so thickly that their weight becomes too much when rain saturates them, and the healthy but overstrained branch comes down with a rending crack! The conditions of tropical rain-forests most closely resemble those under which the group originally developed, and it is for this reason that they are found most widely there.

Ferns that grow in the temperate zone exhibit a similar liking for moist places, but in their case they also prefer it to be cool. These ferns are mostly found in the deep shade and moist coolness of woodland where there is a good quantity of leaf-mould. They also like north-facing cliffs or walls which are perpetually damp with moisture seeping through.

One sizable family has adapted itself to live in perpetual mist or in the constant spray of waterfalls. The fronds of these ferns are unbelievably thin and delicate, and because of this they have been given the very apt name of the 'Filmy' Ferns. They are, of course, totally unable to bear the water-loss of situations drier than those they are accustomed to inhabit. So delicate are they that the glasshouse in which these ferns used to be grown at Kew could not be opened to the public because the changes in conditions caused by the continual opening and shutting of the doors had an adverse effect on the plants. A double-glazed

Right: Polypodium Lineatum, *as it was named in manuscript on another of the elegant drawings in the superb collection of botanical illustrations possessed by the Royal Botanic Gardens at Kew.*
Polypodiaceae *is a very large family, with members in many parts of the world.*
Opposite: The Elk's-Horn or Stag's-Horn Fern (Platycerium) *growing in the Tropical Fern House at Kew. This has been described as amongst the grandest, most beautiful and most extraordinary of all ferns. Certainly its broad forked fronds are quite different in appearance from the minutely divided types illustrated elsewhere in this chapter. The seven species of* Platycerium *are widely distributed in nature and are epiphytic in habit, that is, they perch on other plants but do not draw food from their hosts. Thus in cultivation they thrive in baskets or shallow pans, fastened to a block of wood, in the fork of a tree-branch or in a made-up wall pocket. They have a liking for strong light and under suitable conditions make massive specimens most impressive in appearance, dominating the other ferns in their surroundings.*

Above: John Smith, the first Curator of the living collections of plants grown by Kew, who worked in the Gardens from 1822 until the 1860s, was a Scotsman from Aberdour, Fife. Known as 'Old Jock', he was disliked because he was a stickler for the rules, but his devotion to Kew was never in question. He grew a large number of ferns at Kew and did much basic descriptive work on them.

glasshouse designed so that the effects of public access were kept away from the plants and in which they are not only successfully grown but can be seen by visitors is one of the features that has been added to Kew of late years. There are few other places where they may be seen away from their natural habitat.

Some ferns have carried their desire for moisture to such lengths that they have left the firm anchorage of rock and earth and pushed off from the shore to become floating plants. Water being so easy to get in their case they have not bothered to retain a root system but have adapted some of the leaves on the underside of their floating stem to fulfil the function of roots as well as carrying out their normal task of spore development. These ferns are quite widely spread about the world in waterways where conditions are congenial.

In spite of the apparently inbred desire of most of the members of the fern group to hark back to their origins and to seek moisture and heat, there are some tough species that have gone out into the harsh world of drier conditions and won out. They have done so by various physical adaptations all designed to reduce water loss. Some have covered themselves with wax, others have developed overlapping scales and a third batch has learned to rely on a coating of hairs. In the fern group, however, these are the exception rather than the rule.

The stems of ferns are usually prostrate, either lying on the surface, on rocks, trees and other supports, or burrowing underground. Many are like the common bracken, which has a much-branched creeping underground stem which thrusts up leaves at short intervals so that it soon covers large areas. These types are often very successful. Others have stems which form a mat over the faces of rocky ledges or climb tree trunks. Some

have vertical stems partly underground, and others hark back once more to the past and grow giant stems and leaves like trees.

The most characteristic part of the fern is its leaf. Every country child in Britain has watched with fascination the 'fiddleheads' or 'croziers', as they are variously called, of the new fern leaves as they emerge and unroll from the tip in the spring. Fern leaves are 'compound' in form, having a central leafstalk with leaflets branching off each side which may themselves be subdivided – and the subdivisions again subdivided, producing a lacy complexity of design of great beauty. The leaves vary enormously in size and shape, some attaining a length of eighteen feet and a width of three feet. Some ferns have evolved curious forms for the leaves in their struggle for survival. One climbing fern has leaves of indeterminate length which twine and scramble over other vegetation. Another, a tropical fern, has long forking leaves which are armoured with sharp spines. Patches of this fern are almost impossible to get through. Yet another, the Shoe-String Fern, has long string-like leaves, while a fourth, the Curly-Grass Fern, has short corkscrew leaves like twisted grass.

Ferns enjoyed enormous popularity in Britain in Victorian times. Many ferns are still used as decorative plants in the garden today, both outdoors and under glass, and many make wonderful house plants. But however we grow them, it is impossible to surpass the effect they create in the wild. Ferns make their own unique contribution to the beauty of the plant world. The reader must go seek for himself in the wild places where they grow if he really wishes to know how marvellous they look. But he must not delay too long – these places diminish every year as the inexorable tide of human activity engulfs the wilderness.

Silent Legions

'The firs are ranged in endless dark battalions
On mountain-side and valley, line on line
Waiting the winds. . . .
The mighty trees are grappling to the rock
With every root, preparing for the shock
Of that wild cavalry. . . .'
Eugene Lee-Hamilton

A high spot among recollections of our childhood is the Christmas tree, source of many delights. In northern temperate zones, this is generally a Norway Spruce, like the one erected every year in London's Trafalgar Square to commemorate the help that Great Britain gave Norway against Hitler. Many millions of smaller specimens are raised by nurseries each year to add to the gaiety in countless homes, lit up by fairy lights and surrounded by happy children.

The Norway Spruce is a 'conifer', which means a 'cone-bearing plant'. For most of us, pine-cones will also bring familiar memories of our childhood, when we industriously collected them and perhaps made ornamental things from them, painting them silver or gold. We also pulled them to pieces and in the process discovered, although we did not know it, the characteristic which divides the conifers from plants higher in the scale of evolution. Inside each scale we pulled off we found a seed – not a vessel containing a seed or seeds, but the naked seed itself. This is the key to the distinction. In the most advanced plants in the evolutionary scale the seeds are borne in fruits or pods. The conifers belong, however, to the 'naked-seeded' plants, the gymnosperms.

Conifers produce both male and female cones in the spring when the new shoots and leaves begin to grow. Many cones become woody as they mature, but some remain fleshy. In some species the sexes are carried on different trees and in others the cone is not developed, seed-bearing scales being borne singly on short twigs. The male cone produces great quantities of powdery pollen over a period of about ten days or so, which blows through the forest like sulphur dust. In some cases, such as the genus *Pinus,* the lightness of the pollen grain is accentuated by an air-bladder! Clouds of this pollen have caused alarm in the past when they have descended like a visitation on the panic-striken inhabitants of a remote village. The rain sometimes washes it out of the air in 'sulphur showers', which caused great wonder and speculation. In modern times such occurrences are more likely to arouse commiseration for the poor hay-fever sufferers who so anxiously watch the pollen count!

All but a minute fraction of the pollen so lavishly produced blows away at random in the wind, but a few grains are successfully captured on the sticky surfaces of the female cones, and the process leading to fertilisation begins. This takes a surprisingly long time, often more than a year after the pollen has landed on the cone. The period between pollination and ripening of the seed may be a few months only, though in some kinds of conifer it may be as much as three years. In the genus *Pinus,* for example, the first stage may be seen in May of the first year – a young cone about half an inch long, not yet ripe for

Above: *A conifer weighed down with snow standing sturdily amid the rigours of Norway's winter, hardy symbol of the endurance of the people of the Scandinavian lands.*
Opposite: *One of a number of small line-drawings used to illustrate the* Pinetum Brittanicum, *a lavishly illustrated account of conifers hardy in Great Britain, published in fifty-two parts between 1863 and 1884 by Edward J. Ravenscroft.*

fertilisation, although it may already capture pollen. It rests until the following summer, by which time it has fattened up and become about one and a half inches long. Fertilisation then takes place, and in the third year the cone matures. Some female cones grow to a large size, the longest being that of the Sugar Pine of California, which may reach twenty-six inches.

As we found again when we were children, the seeds we got from the cone were winged and would float down-wind, rotating vigorously if we held them up and let them go. Thus we learnt that some conifers rely on the wind for dispersal of their seeds, as they do for the distribution of their pollen. It all seems very haphazard and wasteful! Those that rely on this method have woody cones. Others, such as the junipers, with fleshy cones, are distributed by animals.

Conifers are plants of the temperate zones of the world, the largest populations being in the northern hemisphere, growing in the regions of long winters and high annual precipitation, where they are the dominant element in the forests, covering enormous tracts of country. The most northerly conifer is the dwarf juniper, which grows beyond the limit where trees will survive. Concentrations of species peculiar to the locality are found in Japan and China, the Himalayas and the North American Pacific coast. Conifers are mainly trees of the hill and mountain, filling the valleys and running up the hillsides to a considerable altitude. They can withstand very low temperatures, but as they approach the limit of tolerable conditions they become more and more stunted and take on the typical ragged and tortured appearance of the inhabitants of the mountain 'tree-line', living their lives out in a perpetual battle with the elements.

Below the tree-line they come into their own. Seizing a foothold on every rock and strip of earth that can possibly be used and in which they can spread their web of roots, they stand together as closely as they can. They hang on to the steepest slopes and lean over the tumbling mountain streams, perching in every crack and crevice of the rocky walls that will hold them, presenting to the artist an infinite variety of scene for his inspiration.

Further down, in level or near level places, they grow taller and more regularly, often in uniform stands with a layer of low shrubs beneath them, the forest floor being covered with liverworts, mosses and lichens. In other places, the closeness cuts off the light and air from the lower branches, which are discarded, leaving their evergreen foliage held aloft by the massive columnar trunks like a canopy far above. In still weather, the silence in such parts of a conifer forest is profound, broken only by the sound of muffled footsteps as they sink deep into the debris of fallen branches and leaves – the accumulation of many years – which comprises the forest floor. In the dim light, vistas in every direction fade off through the endless rows of trunks into the sombre darkness characteristic of the conifer forest. So far as these districts are concerned, the silent ranks of the conifer have taken over the earth. Little else can grow there because of the lack of light. They reign supreme, have done so for immemorial ages and will continue to do so until man, the scourge of nature and the hammer of the biosphere, appears with his axe – then, all will be lost.

Not all the forest is like this. Here and there, by some chance circumstance, a break occurs, and in the small glade the sunlight pours in, a few larger shrubs flourish, and clouds of insects dance in the light while the fragrant odour of resin, which has been with us throughout, seems stronger than under the trees. These places apart, in the wilder areas of the countries of the northern hemisphere, the trees stretch on mile after mile over dale and mountain, up every tributary valley, climbing the sides and scattering off in detachments like soldiers reconnoitring, down to the shores of every lake. Seen from above the tree-line, by those who are hardy enough to make the climb, there are places where they seem like an endless sea, breaking only to let through the island mountain-tops.

The conifers of the southern hemisphere are separated from those of the northern hemisphere by a broad band of tropical forest in which occasional small groups only occur in mountainous regions. They are not found in such extensive congregations as are those of the northern hemisphere. Some kinds are in fact confined to a single island. But nevertheless they are trees of majesty and grandeur, with qualities of their own which dignify the places where they grow. Nor do all conifers live in hilly or mountainous country – some have adapted themselves to live in very wet and even swampy lowland conditions.

The qualities that produce the conifer forests render these trees of great value in the furnishing of gardens and estates. It is true that, originating where they do, in the cloudy moist conditions of the cooler mountainous regions, some of them do not take kindly to the warmer lowlands where enthusiastic gardeners try to grow them. It is, indeed, remarkable that so many of them do so well. It is true also that unwise attempts are

Left centre: Photograph taken from Ravenscroft's Pinetum Brittanicum *of a large Cedar of Lebanon growing in the original habitat of this species. The great forests of this beautiful conifer which covered Mount Lebanon in biblical times are now reduced to a few scattered remnants.*
Left below: Cones of the Stone Pine, taken from A description of the genus Pinus *published by the botanist Aylmer Bourke Lambert in 1803. In his later*

years Lambert lived at Kew.
Left above and opposite above: Conifers above Zermatt, Switzerland.
Opposite below: Line-drawing from Ravenscroft's Pinetum Brittanicum *of the Lawson Cypress, which was discovered in 1854 in northern California. The drawing is of one of four seedlings which were reared in Lawson's nursery at Edinburgh from seed taken from the cones of the original discovery.*

56

The flagpole at Kew Gardens is derived from a Douglas fir presented by the government of British Columbia in 1959. It is the tallest in the world, being 225 feet in length, the tree from which it was cut having been 275 feet high. It is the fourth of its kind to stand in the Royal Botanic Gardens, the first having been presented by Mr Edward Stamp in 1859. This was 159 feet only in height. The flagpole is located on the mound on which formerly stood the Temple of Victory which Sir William Chambers erected for Princess Augusta to commemorate the battle of Minden in 1759. Some living specimens of the Douglas fir grow in the Gardens near the flagpole.

often made to grow many different kinds together in a 'pinetum' – with the natural outcome that some do much better than others and if all are left and no culling takes place a ragged and unequal collection with many indifferent specimens re sults. But it is also true that, although in the forests many conifers shed their lower branches, when they are grown as specimen trees in uncrowded conditions they retain them for much of their life, becoming as they mature tall and slender pyramidal trees of great elegance and distinction.

Not all, however, are of this habit. Some are shrubby in nature but do not lose value on this account since, allowed to form their natural shapes, they grow into very regular and ornamental clumps.

Some conifers have particular virtues of their own. The Monkey-Puzzle tree, for example, found its way in quantity into Great Britain at a time when the carpet-bedding so characteristic of Victorian gardening had become the vogue. Its formal appearance and habit fitted in excellently with the prevailing ideas, and it was extensively planted. The Cedar of Lebanon is another such tree. It carries its branches in a horizontal plane. Grown among other trees with predominantly vertical lines it brings a stillness into the landscape; many examples of it survive in gardens made in the eighteenth century when it was extensively planted.

Another quality of value in the garden which conifers possess is the evergreen nature of their leaves. These stay on the trees for several years – unless, like the Christmas tree, they are brought into the hot and dry atmosphere of the house when, as we discovered towards the end of the Christmas festivities, they start to shed them. We also learnt then that they were needle-shaped and tough, quite unlike the soft and tender green leaves of the broad-leaved trees.

Not all conifers are evergreen. The larch sheds its leaves in the autumn, and the Bald Cypress and the Dawn Redwood throw off their small leaf-bearing twigs in that season too and are leafless during the winter. Similarly, not all conifers have needle-shaped leaves, although this is the commonest form. Some are scale-like, often pressed close to the branch. Others are narrow and pointed, while some are broader and have thin flat blades. All are small, however, even the largest being not more than seven inches long and two inches broad. When

young many conifers have leaves which differ quite markedly from those of the mature tree. Many of the conifers of the southern hemisphere come into this category. In some kinds there is more than one leaf shape, and cases have occurred where trees, although of the same kind, have not been recognised as such.

As most conifers are tall and carry most of their leaves at the top of the tree any water they use has to be pumped a long way. Thus most conifer leaves are thick-skinned and adapted to reduce water loss.

Conifers number in their ranks not only the biggest trees of the world but also the oldest. In the Sierra Nevada mountains of California massive bulks of timber heave themselves into the sky from a base exceeding thirty-five feet in diameter and reach more than 320 feet high. These vast vegetable monsters are the largest living things on earth and are over three thousand years old. Even so, they are mere youngsters compared with another inhabitant of California, the Bristle-Cone Pine of the White Mountain. The age of the oldest of these much smaller but more ancient trees is estimated to be 4600 years, harking back to a time when western civilisation was still confined to that small area in the Middle East where it began, so that one tree has witnessed virtually the whole range of human history.

The seaside relative of the big tree of the Sierra Nevada, the Coastal Redwood, though not quite so bulky as its cousin, grows taller and, at a height approaching four hundred feet, gives pride of place, if at all, only to some giant eucalyptus trees of Australia, which are not conifers. In contrast with these giants must be set the creeping juniper, only one foot tall, and the very smallest of all, a tiny conifer native to New Zealand, with a botanical name nearly as big as itself, *Dacrydium laxifolium* that is only three inches in height!

Top: *Roots of Yew growing over exposed rocks in the Rock Walk at Wakehurst Place, the botanic garden established by Kew in 1965 on National Trust property at Ardingly, near Haywards Heath in Sussex.*
Above: *The Stone Pine, a common tree of Mediterranean lands, growing near Pompeii in Italy.*
Right: *A drawing which appeared in Lambert's* Pinus. *The tree illustrated is a variety often called the Crimean Pine.*
Opposite above: *This scene is in Norway, but it is typical of logging anywhere in the countries where conifers are harvested for lumber.*
Opposite below: *David Douglas, the Scottish plant collector who searched much of western North America for the Royal Horticultural Society in the years 1823 to 1834 and introduced many trees, shrubs and other plants into Great Britain. The Douglas fir is named after him.*

The whole group of conifers is of use economically. The timber lacks the tough fibres of the broad-leaved trees and is classed as softwood, although some kinds are harder than this title would suggest. It is used primarily for constructional work and as pulp for paper-making, though there are a host of other lesser uses. Resin, pitch, turpentine and various oils are also obtained from conifers. The seeds of the Stone Pine of Italy are regarded as a delicacy, and in other parts of the world conifer seeds of various sorts are eaten by man. They are all eaten by animals.

Wherever they may be seen, as single specimens, in groups or in forests, conifers are distinctive and, once recognised, are not easily forgotten. Some of them, grown as individual specimens, have an outstanding beauty of shape and form. The tall unblemished trunks of others have an appeal of their own, often enhanced by attractive bark patterns. The gnarled specimens of the tree-line, hunched and knotted against the ceaseless battering they receive from the wind and the harsh raw cold, have a different kind of beauty, akin to that of courage in adversity. Up in the mountains, the conifer is an essential and characteristic part of innumerable scenes of wild beauty. The quietude and gloom of the sombre conifer forests lower down is alien to man, but its majesty cannot be denied. Here, it can be more easily reached and exploited, and even though in enlightened countries conscious of the value of their forests replacement programmes are followed, in others man is, bit by bit, eating the forests away, the conifers paying the sorry penalty of being one of the groups of plants most useful to man.

The Trappers

'What's this I hear,
....
About the new Carnivora?
Can little plants
Eat bugs and ants?'
Anonymous

Ever since H. G. Wells wrote a story about an orchid which could entice and drug a man with its scent, use its aerial roots to overpower and strangle him, and then feed on his body, there has been an impression abroad that there might somewhere be a man-eating plant. The idea goes further back than this, to the earlier notion entertained by our ancestors, that if you slept under the Upas Tree you would be poisoned and die.

These plants were dangerous enough but their efforts were mild beside those of John Wyndham's Triffids, which set out to destroy mankind and conquer the earth. The film *The Day of the Triffids* opened with a shot of a large and terrifying plant seizing and devouring a custodian in the Palm House at Kew. I am glad to be able to reveal that this scene had no foundation in fact – there are no man eating plants! There are, however, plants which cause a great deal of havoc among the small insect population.

Those of us who are gardeners are concerned, one way or another, with finding methods which will stop insects eating plants. In the case of the carnivorous plants, the world of vegetation is hitting back. The process is reversed. The plants eat the insects instead of the insects eating the plants!

It is a pity that we cannot enlist the activities of these plants on our side to help to eradicate some of our insect pests. A biological agent which attacks another which has become a nuisance can often be invaluable for control purposes. Unfortunately, the carnivorous plants are rather too static in their approach to the problem to be of service. The truth is that such plants, compared with the Triffids, are a lackadaisical lot! There are no waving tentacles (except on a microscopic scale) or writhing roots creeping inexorably towards the prey, transfixed in helpless terror. In fact there is no positive approach at all. They simply sit and wait for the unwary insect to wander into their trap! This chapter, which reveals the carnivorous plants for the modest characters they are, scratching an honest living in adverse circumstances by snapping up a few unconsidered insects, might well, therefore, be sub-titled 'The Truth about the Triffids'!

The most remarkable of these plants, which Charles Darwin called 'the most wonderful plant in the world', is the Venus' Flytrap, which grows on the coastal plain and adjacent hills of North and South Carolina. Unremarkable in its general appearance – it is a small perennial herb with a basal rosette of leaves and a flowering stalk about a foot in length usually bearing up to a dozen or fifteen white flowers – it possesses most fearsome looking toothed leaves, with which it catches its prey. If a rash fly, attracted by nectar, wanders between the two halves of the leaf and happens to touch some sensitive hairs on the inside, a mechanism is triggered off which causes (and here

the Triffid strain emerges!) the two halves to snap together. The victim is trapped inside, cannot get out because of the spiny teeth interlocked across the gap and is digested at leisure. When the jaws open again nothing but the skeleton remains.

The sarracenias, also natives of North America, catch their prey in a different way. They consist of a basal rosette with long flower stalks, but the flowers are often somewhat more showy, each being several inches across and yellow, greenish-yellow or dark red in colour. It is in the leaves, however, that the great difference lies. These are tubular and horn shaped, with a lid arching over the opening to keep out rain or unwanted matter. Insects are attracted to the mouth by nectar. Moving innocently over the hairs in search of the delectable liquid, they find when they are satiated that the hairs are pointing in the wrong direction to enable them to get out. Their efforts to do so inevitably bring them on to a smooth and lubricated part of the throat. Struggling ineffectually, they slide down this into the gaping cavity below and are lost for ever! The bottom of the leaf contains digestive juices which make easy work of their soft parts, while the horny remains accumulate. Success, however, brings a penalty, for birds often split open the leaves to get at maggots which develop in the undigested debris.

The darlingtonia, which grows in wet meadows of the coastal area of California and southern Oregon, behaves like the sarracenia but looks far more menacing. The tops of the leaves are hoodlike instead of open, the two projecting portions of the landing ramp under the hood looking for all the world like a forked tongue which has just flicked out, the whole being reminiscent of a cobra's head poised to strike!

The sarracenias and the darlingtonia are 'pitcher-plants', but this name is more familiarly applied to a genus of vinelike shrubby plants which grows on the other side of the world. The nepenthes are found mainly in the region of Borneo, though there are some as far afield as Madagascar, tropical Asia and north Australia. They creep along the soil or climb over their neighbours in the warm rain-forests but are also found in the savannah land or even on dry hillsides. Their leaves are

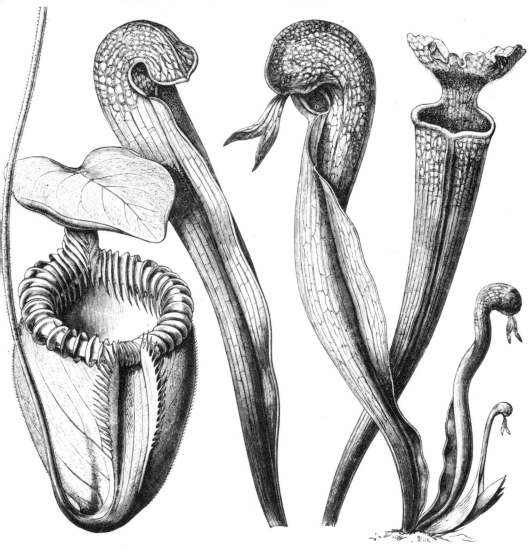

The Victorian naturalist, Alfred Russell Wallace, was greatly impressed with pitcher plants when he visited Borneo in 1855–6. 'The wonderful pitcher plants . . .', he wrote in The Malay Archipelago, 'here reach their greatest development. Every mountain top abounds with them, running along the ground, or climbing over shrubs and stunted trees, their elegant pitchers hanging in every direction. Some of these are long and slender . . . others are broad and short. Their colours are green, variously tinted and mottled with red or purple.'

Opposite: The Venus' Flytrap, Dionoea muscipula, *from* Buchoz'Histoire Universelle *(1773). The speed with which the halves of its toothed leaves snap together to trap prey makes it seem almost animal.*
Left: Various pitchers, from an engraving in the Natural History of Plants *by Anton Kerner von Marilaun.*
Below left: Pitchers of Heliamphora nutans, *a rare carnivorous plant.*

modified into tendrils which, once they have performed their primary function of getting a hold on something, go on to develop pitcher-like containers at their tips. These may be small but are often of substantial size, some having a capacity of as much as a pint and being twenty inches in length. They trap their prey in very much the same way as the sarracenias but rely on a crumbly waxen surface within the upper half of the pitcher, which provides no foothold at all for the struggling victim, as the final measure to complete their fell purpose.

The sundews have yet another method of trapping prey. They are variable in appearance: some have a basal rosette, while others climb or carry their leaves in the air, the leaves being broad in some species, narrow or even wirelike in others. All, however, catch insects in the same way – a way which is entirely their own. The flytrap or pitcher plant relies on the insect being attracted in and then merely prevents it getting out. The sundew goes further. As soon as the victim sets foot on the leaf, flexible tentacles, with which the upper surface is covered exude mucilage and (perhaps H. G. Wells was not so far from the truth even though it all happens on a microscopic scale!) he finds he has great difficulty in moving. His struggles only stimulate more secretion, and he is very soon hopelessly tied down. The tentacles gradually shift the carcase towards the middle of the leaf, and in the broader-leafed species the edges of the leaf also bend round the prey, which is then digested. In a week or so the process, which is comparatively slow, is completed, the leaf reopens, the trap is reset, and once more the drops of mucilage on the leaf glands shine like dew in the sun – the effect that gives the plant its name – awaiting the next victim.

The method used by the butterworts to catch insects resembles that of the sundew, although it is not precisely the same. The comparatively large leaves of this plant are always borne in

a rosette which lies flat on the ground. The whole of their upper surface becomes covered with mucilage which gives the leaves the 'buttery' feeling from which their name comes, each leaf being a kind of shallow pan with a turned up edge. An insect landing on the leaf stimulates the secretion of the mucilage and, as in the sundew, the victim finds he cannot move. Small insects are completely covered while larger ones are pushed towards the deeper centre as the edges of the leaf curl up. Once the victim is immobilised and dies the juices get to work to digest it.

Both the sundews and the butterworts are inhabitants of bogs and wetlands. Neither has very spectacular flowers, the sundew sending up a stalk bearing up to twenty white, pink or even red flowers which open only when the sun is out, while the flowers of the butterwort are like those of a violet – hence the alternative name of 'Bog Violet'.

Although not the most spectacular of the carnivorous plants, chiefly because of their small scale – the palm for this must go to the Venus' Flytrap – the bladderworts have a claim to be the most interesting, because they are mostly aquatic, and also, perhaps, to be the most successful, since they are spread very widely around the world. They are not very large plants, some being almost microscopic while the biggest does not usually exceed a yard in length. Those which are not fully aquatic usually lie on wet mud, sand or moss with only their flower stalks above the ground. None of them possesses roots, and the leaves are finely divided.

For a long time it was thought that the bladder-like swellings on the bladderwort leaves were merely floats to keep the plant on top of the water. It was, however, discovered that, far from being so innocent in intent, they were peculiarly cunning traps, set to catch the passing small crustacean or other tiny organism as it unsuspectingly approached. The bladders are pear-shaped and attached to the stalk at one side, having a mouth at the narrow end. There are bristles down the side and antennae at the mouth which form a kind of directing passage for the victim. A trap-door hangs over the mouth, which has, on the outside, glands secreting nectar and mucilage, together with some stiff bristles which are the triggering mechanism. The small aquatic animal comes looking for the nectar, touches the bristles, the door swings free, the sides of the bladder move outwards, water rushes in through the open door carrying the animal in with it, the sides and door move in again, and all is over! The animal cannot get out again and is swiftly digested.

No matter how ingenious a device may be, evolutionary change eventually finds an answer to it. The maggots which the birds find in the sarracenias are the larvae of a fly which has found a way of combating the digestive juices and can live happily in the pitchers. A mosquito has also developed the faculty of living within the pitchers in the same way. Similarly, some microscopic organisms thrive within the traps of the bladderwort. For these species it is a remarkable fact that the devices are not, as intended, a place of burial, but of birth!

Why do plants choose such a method of finding their food? Surely it would be simpler to root in the soil and draw the necessary nutriment from that source as most other plants do? We do not really know what has induced these plants to seek animal food, but we suspect that in marginal conditions the additional nitrogen from the animal proteins may mean the difference between survival and extinction. Some carnivorous plants, however, live quite well without their insect food, and it must, of course, be remembered that all of them are green plants manufacturing food from sunlight, water and carbon dioxide and do not depend wholly upon insect food for nourishment. Whatever their reasons for adopting their mode of life, they are a curious and intriguing part of the plant kingdom in which the natural order of things seems to be upside down.

Opposite: A pitcher plant, Nepenthes *species, growing at Kew. A glasshouse solely devoted to these interesting plants has been maintained at the Royal Botanic Gardens for many years. There is a particular fascination about carnivorous plants and the first question of many visitors to Kew is to ask where these are in the Gardens. Unfortunately, most of these plants are small and indistinguished, so those who see them for the first time are often disappointed. The* Nepenthes, *being larger, are, however, rather more impressive than the others.*

Left: A South African sundew, Drosera capensis. *Unlike the sundew of Great Britain, whose leaves form a flat rosette, this species holds its leaves in the air. The dew-like drops of mucilage which give the plant its name can be seen on the hairs.*

Below left: A species of Nepenthes *growing in the Seychelles.*

Below: The Butterwort, or Bog Violet, seen here displaying its most attractive flowers in a drawing of Victorian times from Curtis's Botanical Magazine.

False Lovers

*'See on that floweret's velvet breast
How close the busy vagrant lies;
I sought the living bee to find
And found the picture of a bee.'*
John Langhorne

In the romantic imaginings of the novelist of high society, the heroine almost always has an exotic and expensive orchid pinned to her evening gown, and, if we are lucky enough to have an illustration, we may even see an artist's impression of the flower so worn. Apart from the few who, in life, move in such circles, this is about as near as most of us get to the real thing – unless, of course, we take a trip to a garden like Kew. Even there we are not likely to see the showiest blooms, because these are hybrids, specially bred by a highly skilled industry for a lucrative reward willingly paid by the wealthy.

The orchid industry is, indeed, one of the most advanced in methods of propagation. In the production of flowers for profit, the shorter the time that elapses between the establishment of a new plant and the opening of its flowers, the saleable part, the lower the overheads and the greater the profit. Production can be increased by dividing up the plant or in some species by taking cuttings of it, but the number that can be raised in these ways from one plant is limited. Orchids can also be raised from seed, but the seed is very small, lives for a few months only at normal temperatures and in many cases germinates very slowly. The seeds have no food reserves and rely in nature upon a fungus which grows in intimate relation with them for their food supply. Careful treatment along precise lines is therefore required for success to be obtained, and even then the orchid grown from seed is, in the case of hybrids, not necessarily identical with the parent.

For a long time orchid-growers got over these difficulties as best they could, but since about the middle 1960s a method of propagation has come into use which has the advantage not only of being quicker and more prolific but of producing plants identical with the parent. This is of immense value when it is desired to perpetuate rarities with desirable characteristics. The method used consists of taking a small portion of the growing tissue of a plant and, by laboratory treatment, inducing it to produce tiny individual plants which will develop into normal adults.

However skilful orchid-growers become in propagating new plants and reducing the cost of producing the flowers, orchids are never likely to become common garden plants. It is true that some of the hardy orchids that grow in cool bogs and woods in the temperate zones may in suitable situations be grown as garden plants, and it is also true that some others will survive as house plants, but the most attractive kinds come from the warm rain-forests which hang on the slopes of the mountains and hills in the hotter parts of the world. The habitat and environment they enjoy can be reproduced only with difficulty in temperate lands. They are always likely to remain, as they have been since they first grew popular, the preserve of the specialist gardener with a little more money to spare for his hobby than most.

The expense of growing orchids is not the reason why they are regarded, by general acclaim, as the aristocrats of the plant world. The flowers of many of them are of such breathtaking delicacy of colour, texture and complexity that it would be an insensitive person who was not moved by their beauty. One

Left: *Plate from an old work captioned* Catachaetum recurvatum, *showing an orchid of curious green-yellow colouring and unusual shape.*

Above: *Illustration from the* Gardener's Chronicle *of* Cattleya gigas *captioned 'Sir Trevor Lawrence's specimen' – featured separately by the magazine because it was a well-grown floriferous plant.*

Opposite: *One of the numerous attractive orchids found in South America,* Zygopetalum lindeniae. *This plant illustrates well the delicacy of colouring and bizarre shapes of these most* showy and sophisticated of all flowers – the apparatus by which the plant lures on the desired pollinator to do its work. Interest in orchids has never flagged since methods were discovered of cultivating them, and such is the range of colour and shape that can be produced by hybridisation of flowers such as this one that interest in the family is likely to grow rather than diminish, particularly as modern methods of propagation may make plants more easily available. Many thousands of species are grown at Kew and can be seen on display as they come into flower in the glasshouses open to the public.

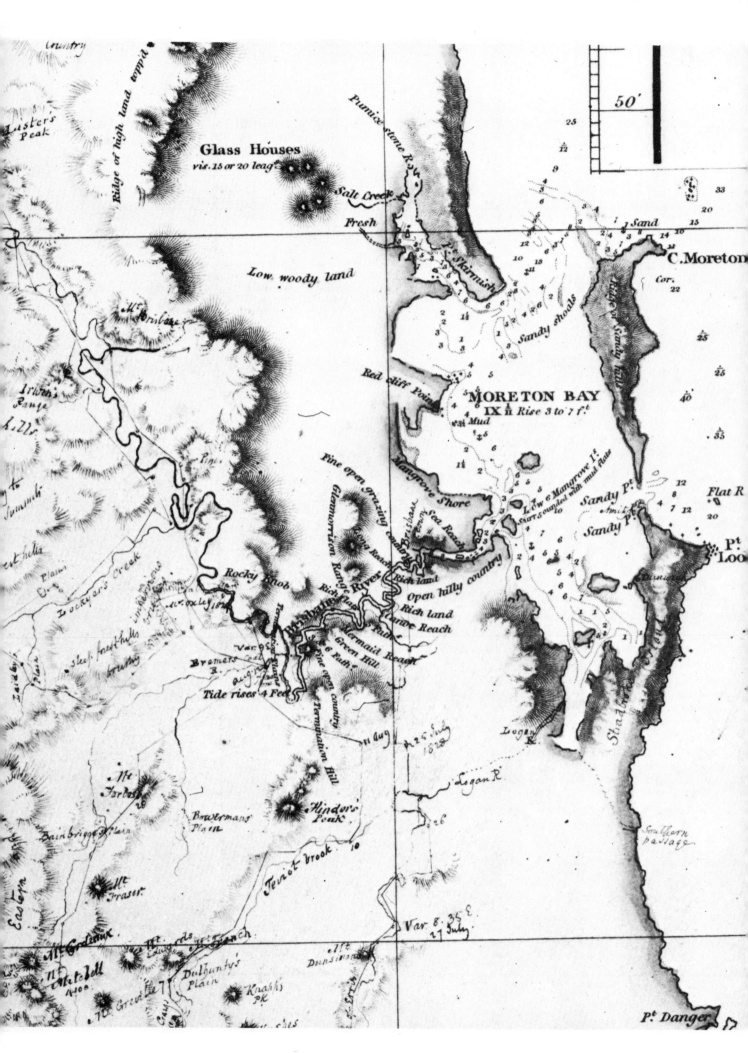

Allan Cunningham first made four circumnavigations of the continent of Australia and then a number of journeys to the lands west of the mountains which cut off the eastern coast from the interior. His collecting journeys, made with a horse and cart and little companionship, did much to enlighten the early settlers on what lay beyond the formidable Dividing Range. During the course of his explorations he collected and sent to Kew many orchids.

flower often has as many as six or seven different hues. Although blue is not common and there is no true black, the nearest being deep purple-brown, all other colours can be found, in an immense variety of shades. Other families may possess members with flowers of similar beauty, but none surpasses the orchids in variety and numbers of species with attractive flowers.

The beauty of orchid flowers is not, as one might expect, always accompanied by pleasurable scent, although some are very fragrant. A good many have no detectable smell at all, but some tropical species have odours which, to the human nose, are not at all pleasant; some are even positively offensive – but then, they are not designed to attract the human organism: they have a different idea in mind! Their aim is to lure an insect pollinator, and not any insect pollinator, but in most cases, one particular kind (and even sex) of insect. The whole design of the orchid flower, which is among the most complex in the plant world, is ingeniously contrived to entice the favoured insect to enter the flower and, when within, to follow a particular course so that any pollen it is carrying comes into contact with and is deposited on the female surface, the flower's own pollen being loaded on to the insect for it to carry away.

The chief pollinators are butterflies and moths, but many orchids are pollinated by bees, wasps and ants and some by flies. Humming birds and even snails are the agents in other cases. The beautiful exterior of the flower is irregular in shape, with one of the petals enlarged and converted into a 'lip', usually more highly-coloured than the rest, which may be flat and is often fringed, spurred or lobed and may also be pouch-shaped. This presents an inviting landing-place for the prospecting insect. The outside of the flower is, however, merely 'the label on the box'. Inside is one of the distinctive features of the orchid which marks it out from related families. The stamens (male) and the stigma (female) which in others are separate are, in the orchid, combined in what is technically known as the 'column'. Most of the stamens have disappeared, leaving only one, the pollen being tied together in pockets by elastic thread to form sticky masses called 'pollinia'. The willing insect blunders in, looking for the nectary from which to drink the sweet honey, finds that in most cases it has to bite into or drill

the tissue to obtain it and in so doing bumps its pollen-laden self (having previously visited another flower of the same species) against the stigma, sheds the pollen on it while it does so, and then backs out, brushing off the pollinia and carrying them away with it – and lo! the trick is done: and very neatly too, since the method ensures cross-pollination.

Were the bright colours of the flowers, the peculiar odours which some emit and the attraction of honey in the nectaries the only things on which orchids relied to attract their pollinators, there would be nothing to mark out their gifts in this direction above those of other families. They have, however, perfected another quality, that of mimicry, which is quite astonishing in its efficacy. This has been taken so far in some kinds that the insects visit the plant not in search of food but sexual excitement! In an act called by botanists 'pseudo-copulation' the insect is attracted to the plant by the 'lip' of the flower, which has modifications simulating the female insect, and is induced to engage in movements, clearly copulatory in intent, against the 'column'; while so doing, it pollinates the stigma and captures the pollinia! Once again, the orchid is ahead of its rivals.

Some may find it very hard to visualise how precisely integrated systems of life such as those of the orchid could come about by the random chances of evolution. The orchid relies upon a fungus which grows in intimate relationship with its roots to find its food supply; it has an equally precise relationship with the insect which pollinates it – and also, for good measure, with the environment in which it grows. These arrangements are so narrowly adapted to a particular set of circumstances that they defy belief that they could have come about in any way other than by special creation. It requires a distinct effort of the imagination to accept that this state of affairs is the result of an evolutionary process, that along the line from the primitive undifferentiated flower there were intermediate steps, cruder and less well adapted forms, of which only the most successful survived and continued to change until the present highly sophisticated arrangement was reached. The human mind reaches instinctively for the idea of someone consciously developing a plan and is uncomfortable with the notion that such a specialised end product as the portrayal of an insect so faithfully as to fool another insect of the same species could come about without someone directing the process and making a conscious decision to strive for it. The 'record of the rocks' does not help, as fossils that can be placed without

Opposite: Oncidium praetextum.
Below left: Cypripedium pubescens.
Below centre: Rigidella orthantha *at Kew and, beneath it,* Sobralia infundibuligera.
Right: Dendrobium nobile.

dispute in the evolutionary progression of orchids have not so far been discovered. There is, however, no other explanation as plausible and no option for us but to jump the credibility gap.

The remarkable nature of the flowers of the orchid tends to distract attention from the rest of the plant, which also has some interesting features. Orchids are nearly all perennial and herbaceous, that is, they do not normally have woody stems, though some become shrubby and others grow like vines. The kinds which grow in temperate lands are mainly rooted in the earth (these are called 'terrestrial' orchids) and have a swollen part of the stem or storage tuber to enable them to withstand dry periods, but a very large number of those which grow in the rain-forests of the warmer countries have a different mode of existence. They grow lodged on the trunk or branches of trees. Their tissues do not penetrate the tree or unite with their host. They do not draw sustenance from it and are thus not parasites, nor do they help it in any way, merely using it as a suitable perch. Plants which adopt such a habit are termed 'epiphytes'.

The epiphytic way of living requires some adaptation to meet conditions different from those experienced by plants rooted in the earth. The roots which grapple the plant on to the host tree cannot draw moisture from the soil or from the tree itself, but

69

from these roots branch roots are developed that absorb food from the humus which collects in the spaces between the plant and its support. Other roots that hang freely from the plant in festoons have been developed with the capacity to extract water from the air. The outer skin of these 'aerial' roots is dead and acts as an assimilating water jacket supplying water to the green tissue within. As the humidity is very high in the rain-forests where the orchids live, plentiful supplies of water are usually available for these roots to draw upon. When the dry season does come, many orchids drop their leaves (although they may still flower) and rely for survival on swollen storage organs at the base called 'pseudobulbs', one of which is usually formed each year. Others retain the leaves and use them for the same purpose, so that they become thick and fleshy.

The leaves of orchids are not a particularly conspicuous part of the plant. They have parallel veins and may be many or single, sometimes being absent altogether. They are often quite fleshy. Orchids vary greatly in size, from a minute little plant only a quarter of an inch in height to one which reaches twenty feet. Similarly, some have tiny but perfectly formed flowers barely one-sixteenth of an inch across while others may be as large as ten inches in diameter. Apart from their value as ornamental plants, which is the basis of a world-wide luxury industry in which vast sums of money are involved, orchids have few uses. Only one, the vanilla orchid, supplies a useful product to the modern commercial market. The vanilla flavouring is derived from the cured unripe pods of the plant, which is vine-like in habit.

The orchid family contains some oddities. There are some orchids which feed wholly on dead organic matter and are thus, in a sense, scavengers. These have no green leaves and often no roots, their food being absorbed directly by a fleshy underground stem. Some very strange kinds found in Australia are subterranean in habit, and a few have adapted themselves in part to live in water. Some of the family are able to put up with very cold conditions, even growing in Greenland or high up

Right: A handsome cultivated variety of Cattleya named 'Rex O'Brien', drawn by the botanical artist Matilda Smith for Curtis's Botanical Magazine. Cattleya is probably the showiest orchid genus.
Below: Drawing by W. H. Fitch of Oncidum longipes, a dwarf-growing but showy species from the Organ Mountains of Brazil. The lip of the flower is deep yellow and blood red, the rest greenish-yellow streaked with reddish-brown.
Opposite: Vanda tricolor in the Orchid House at Kew. This impressive orchid, whose flowers are white outside, the petals being a pale yellow spotted with brownish-red and the lip rose-magenta and white, is a native of Java. Many handsome varieties have been bred from it.

near the snow line of the Andes. Others will tolerate the salt spray of the sea-coast, while yet others will flourish in a climate where they are baked dry for several months each year, in contrast with those which prefer bog conditions. Possessing both vigour and exceptional adaptability, the orchid family has found that it can grow anywhere except in the frozen polar regions. But, as already indicated, although it grows in quite considerable numbers elsewhere its first love is the warm rain-forest, and it is there that most of its kind are found.

Although the great popularity of orchids dates back little more than 150 years, our ancestors knew a little of their local kinds and, as is usual, 'the Greeks had a word' for them. They were struck, in the kinds they knew, with the underground part, which they found consisted of two tubers resembling nothing so much as testicles. Not being prudish, they adopted the Greek word for testicle, *orchis*, for their plants, and it has stuck to the family ever since.

From this resemblance, orchids were called such names as 'Dog's Stones', 'Fool's Stones', and so on and acquired a

reputation for being effective in sex matters. William Turner set out the belief of his time in his *Herbal*. He called the plant 'Adder's Grasse'. 'There are divers kinds of orchis,' he said, 'which are called in Latin "testiculus", that is, a stone . . . . The root of it, when it is sodden enough, is eatable as bulbus is. They write of this herb that if the greater root be eaten of men it maketh men children . . . . This is also told of it, that the women of Thessalia gave it with goat's milk to provoke the pleasure of the body . . . .'

Shakespeare knew the orchid of English meadows, calling it 'long purples', but in his time the exploration of the plant world was only just beginning. Orchids, indeed, were somewhat late in becoming an object of study for British botanists as the first one from abroad did not arrive in Britain until the eighteenth century was well advanced. When they did begin to be sent in by collectors there was little success in cultivating them as the conditions under which they grew were not understood. A few were got to flower, some at Kew, before they died, so that their beauty could be seen, and their reputation began to grow. But, as the eighteenth century drew to a close, skill in cultivating them still largely eluded gardeners.

During the Napoleonic wars in the first years of the new century little further progress was made, but in 1818 a showy

Above: Early Victorian orchid illustration from the botanical journal run by Sir Joseph Paxton, designer of the Crystal Palace – Paxton's Magazine of Botany. *Paxton was head gardener to the Duke of Devonshire at Chatsworth.*

Above right: Illustration from The Garden *of a striking orchid, called the 'Siberian Lady's Slipper'. The large lip, which resembles a comfortable piece of footwear and gives the flower its name, is characteristic of many orchids.*

Cattleya was seen in England which was so attractive that it aroused considerable interest. Others were imported, and progress began to be made in getting them to grow. At Kew collections of orchids received from collectors in Brazil had mostly died. A young foreman of the time, who was later to be a famous Curator of Kew, John Smith, sets out why no success had been achieved. 'The whole', he says, 'had been potted in common soil, and the pots plunged to the rim in a tan bed, within a few feet of the glass roof, without being shaded from the summer sun, the hothouse being heated by a common flue [heating by hot water pipes had not then been invented] the dry heat of which not being congenial to the growth of epiphytic plants . . . they were in a deplorable state, dead or dying.' When, in 1823, a collection of orchids was received from Australia, John Smith tried something different. The plants were put in a different house 'in loose turfy soil interspersed with small portions of stems of trees'. The method was somewhat more successful and 'many of them grew freely'. Shortly afterwards, further progress was made. 'Between the years 1823 and 1825, a considerable number of species was received from Trinidad . . . all of which were epiphytal.' Many of them were sent 'growing on portions of branches as cut from the trees' and were accompanied by instructions 'as to how they should be treated'. The problem still was by no means fully solved however. Many orchids brought to Kew still failed to survive and experience was similar elsewhere.

As soon as they began to be grown a craze for orchids began among the rich, and fantastic prices were paid for individual plants. One of the principal enthusiasts in the early days was the Duke of Bedford. His collection was given to Queen Victoria in 1843 and she passed it on to Kew. The results that followed an account by Sir Joseph Hooker of an experience in

The blue Vanda *orchids in their natural southeast Asian habitat are magnificent. In certain places they are not uncommon, but their colour is variable, some forms being darker and more vivid than others. The darker are generally preferred, some being almost ultramarine in colour.*

The plants seem generally to grow larger in the wild than in cultivation, perhaps because the conditions under which they grow best are rarely reproduced exactly. As many as forty-five perfect blooms have been seen on a single wild plant. It is not surprising therefore that Sir Joseph Hooker was enraptured with this orchid when he saw it in India and tried to send a large consignment to Kew – unfortunately unsuccessfully.

the Khasia Hills of India give a good idea of how matters now developed. A particularly beautiful blue orchid grew in these hills. Sir Joseph wrote in his *Journal*: 'Near the village of Larnac oak woods are passed in which "the blue orchid" grows in profusion. . . . This beautiful orchid is at present attracting great attention from its high price, beauty and difficulty of cultivation . . . .' He then describes the climatic conditions and points out that what the plant was experiencing in nature was far different from the treatment it was being given at home. He continues: 'We collected seven men's loads of this superb plant for the Royal Gardens at Kew, but owing to unavoidable accidents and difficulties few specimens reached England alive. A gentleman, who sent his gardener with us to be shown the locality, was more successful. He sent one man's load to England on commission and, although it arrived in a poor state, sold for £300, the individual plants fetching prices varying from £3 to £10. Had all arrived alive they would have cleared £1,000. An active collector, with the facilities I possessed might easily clear from £2,000 to £3,000 in one season by the sale of Khasia orchids.' In due course these remarks became known in India. Businessmen were quick to seize the opportunity and took up the export of blue orchids. Eventually the

Below: *This engraving from a Victorian horticultural journal shows an orchid with large and showy flowers of the kind that breeders have so successfully used to produce improved cultivated varieties.*
Opposite: *Engraving from the* Gardener's Chronicle *of 15 April 1880 of a plant of the orchid* Cymbidium eburneum. *The fine flowering specimen from which the engraving was made was presumably a single plant. This orchid, which has white, creamy-white or ivory-white flowers, is exceptionally fragrant, an additional attraction that many orchids do not possess. The* Cymbidium, *of which there are some fifty species, are natives of southeast Asia and are found as far south as Australia.*

governments of Assam and Burma had to intervene to prevent denudation of the forests – an early example of conservation legislation.

As the century progressed and it became obvious that there was much money to be made collectors were sent out specially to gather orchids, and the havoc they wrought now seems incredible. Whole areas were denuded of trees and appeared as if they had been ravaged by a forest fire. It is recorded, for example, that in one search in Colombia for a particular orchid ten thousand plants were collected, four hundred trees having been felled to reach them. As one area was stripped the collector moved on to another, stalking across the vegetation step by step like a giant plague. All sorts of subterfuges were adopted to keep favoured locations a secret, even to the extent of collecting plants and then destroying the remainder so that others would not find them and their rarity value would be increased. An unfortunate result of this excessive secrecy and the faulty methods of cultivation was that many orchids which perhaps flowered once on arrival in England and were then lost could not easily be traced, little or nothing being known about their place of origin. Many years often went by before they were found again and reintroduced. One well-known case was that of a striking *Cypripedium* from the Himalayas which was exhibited at the Royal Horticultural Society's show in the 1850s but afterwards died. Although a reward of £1,000 was offered for its rediscovery, it was not found again until 1904.

The annals of garden history are fortunately comparatively free from instances of the evil effects of unbridled human greed. This case of the orchids is, perhaps, the worst example. Fortunately it is now over – to be replaced, sadly, by something infinitely worse. Where the orchid collectors looked only for one family and did the damage incidentally, now in many areas the tropical rain-forest is being wholly removed in pursuit of a notion, not infrequently mistaken, that the land can be profitably exploited in other ways. When the rain-forest goes, its orchids go for ever.

A portrait made in 1848 of John Lindley, the eminent botanist who was contemporary with and friend and rival of Sir William Jackson Hooker, the first Director of Kew when it became a state garden in 1841, following the report of a group led by Lindley. He served the Royal Horticultural Society for many years and was an expert on orchids. His collection of dried orchid specimens is preserved at Kew.

Fortune Hunters

'Sweete bands, take heed lest you ungently bind,
Or with your strictness make too deepe a printe. . . .'
Sir John Davies

The biggest climbing plant ever known must certainly have been the beanstalk up which Jack climbed in 'Jack and the Beanstalk', since that was large enough to have a giant's castle and a giant on top! Such a large climber would have needed a very stout support up which to climb, but the story is conveniently silent upon what this was!

Climbing plants have one object only in adopting their mode of life. It is not, of course, the provision, in their upper parts, of homes for giants! All green plants need sunlight to carry out photosynthesis of food in their cells, and climbing plants are out to ensure that at least part of their body system is carried up to where the light is strongest. All their actions tend towards this end, and they are ruthless in pursuit of their aim. In their climb they must use other plants, and in doing so they not infrequently cause damage and death.

As it is shade which plants dread most, and to avoid which they climb, it follows that where vegetation is thickest, and the shade is greatest, the largest number of climbers will occur. Plants grow most thickly in the tropical areas of the world and it is in the tropics that the largest climbers are found and the greatest variety of climbing plants.

In the most mature parts of the tropical forests competition from the great trees and their overspreading canopy reduces the vegetation on the forest floor or in the lower parts to those plants which, like the ferns, have accustomed themselves to the gloom; even the climbers, unless they established themselves when the trees were younger, have difficulty in surviving. Where, however, there is the slightest thinning, on the edge of glades, where trees have fallen, on the margin, or anywhere where there is an opening, the climber comes into its

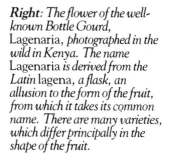

Right: The flower of the well-known Bottle Gourd, Lagenaria, *photographed in the wild in Kenya. The name* Lagenaria *is derived from the Latin* lagena, *a flask, an allusion to the form of the fruit, from which it takes its common name. There are many varieties, which differ principally in the shape of the fruit.*

Above left: Passiflora quadrangularis, *a colourful Passion Flower cultivated for its delicious fruit, the Granadilla, shown here in an illustration from the* Flore des Antilles *by F. R. de Tussac.*
Above centre: The flowers of Ivy, Hedera helix, *more commonly associated with the darkness of ruins than with this sunlit scene.*

Opposite: A plate from Illustrations of Himalayan Plants *by J. D. Hooker showing three species of attractive Himalayan climbers, named in the picture as* Codonopsis, *which W. H. Fitch, the famous botanical artist who for many years worked closely with the Hookers, combined into one graceful and ornamental pattern to fill the page almost completely.*

Plate XV

own. It is difficult to convey in words what the forest is like at such points. Plant piles upon plant in one grand heap of vegetation, scrambling one over the other in apparent vast confusion right up to and over the top of the trees, twining and grappling with each other so that it is impossible to distinguish one plant from another. The stem that here climbs up from the ground, a foot or two away is lost from view, and what root eventually gives sustenance to which flower is impossible to tell!

The greatest climbers of the forest are immense woody plants called lianas. The name does not refer to any particular genus or family but to these giant climbers generally as a group. As they climb, inextricably mixed with one another and with other plants, they here hang free in festoons, elsewhere span the gap between tree and tree like rope bridges, and there climb up in a pyramid of vegetation over an ancient tree with their topmost foliage thrust up triumphantly over their host into the light and air of the freer world above the forest. In places where they have been long established and have grown up with the trees on which they have climbed, they shed their lower leaves and stretch like ropes – or, indeed, great hawsers – from the ground to the tops of the trees. Many become flattened, twisted or distorted in other ways by the tensions which develop in the process of climbing and competing with their hosts and neighbours.

Among the great climbers are many not quite so large or

R. T. Günther, in Oxford Gardens *(1912), tells of a climbing plant which liked port – a trait not perhaps too unexpected in a plant of a university town, where the noble beverage circulates freely around High Table. 'The roots of the ivy', he writes, 'penetrated the vault of an adjoining wine-cellar and, after branching about in the sawdust where the bottles lay, made for a cork through which some moisture was oozing, entered the bottle, drank up all the port, and then filled the bottle entirely with a matted tangle of roots all growing in search of more of the ambrosial liquor, but unable to get through the glass!'*

SIR JOHN HILL, M.D.
KNIGHT OF THE POLAR STAR.
First Superintendant of the Royal Gardens at Kew.

vigorous, and a distinction, convenient but not really botanical, is sometimes drawn between those which have a woody stem thick and rigid enough to allow them, if the worst comes to the worst, to support themselves if no other support is available and others which, while woody, cannot make bushes without support and, lacking it, writhe impotently along the ground, unable to achieve the height they crave. At one end the latter shade off into the great climbers and at the other into those without woody tissue which must have support from outside to climb.

Lest you should think that tropical climbers produce no more than a tangle of green-leaved stems, a giant green hedge walling in the deep forest, or, within that forest, the semblance of the

Opposite: *A climbing shrub entitled in* Curtis's Botanical Magazine *of 1808, from which this illustration is taken,* Clematis cylindrica, *the 'Long-Flowered Virgin's Bower'.*
Above: *Portrait of Sir John Hill, bearing the claim, in the title underneath, that he was 'First Superintendent of the Royal Gardens at Kew'. Hill's function at Kew in the early years of the botanic garden is not known, but he was probably a protégé of Lord Bute. In 1768 he published a* Hortus Kewensis *listing the plants in the garden. Hill was a colourful character with a prodigious literary output, mostly worthless, though it did contain a small but genuine contribution to advancement.*

Below: *The colourful fruit of* Ruthalicia eglandulosa, *a climber from Ghana, with a closely-coiled tendril.*
Right: *Illustration by W. H. Fitch from* Curtis's Botanical Magazine *of a showy climber,* Clerodendron thomsonae. *Kew first received a living specimen of this plant from the Royal Botanic Garden, Edinburgh, in January 1862, it having been sent there by the Reverend W. C. Thomson, a missionary at Old Calabar on the west coast of Africa, during the previous year. The plant was named after Thomson's deceased wife. Its highly decorative appearance and willingness to flower have earned it a firm place in the affections of gardeners.*

The clematis of the English hedgerows, Clematis vitalba, used to be called 'Traveller's Joy'. Its flowers are greenish-white and the seeds are furnished with a tuft of silvery down which hangs on the bush for most of the winter, giving it its second common name, 'Old Man's Beard'. Yet a third name for it is much more poetic – 'Virgin's Bower'. Country people in the past are said to have used clematis instead of pipes for smoking, and beggars used to utilise the leaves to produce ulcers in order to excite pity and obtain alms. It has a number of very beautiful large-flowered relatives of great use as garden plants.

Right: *A pretty twining shrub from China named* Akebia quinata, *here reproduced from an illustration by W. H. Fitch in Curtis's Botanical Magazine. Living plants were introduced from the wild by Robert Fortune, who collected for the Royal Horticultural Society in the 1840s, but had previously been known in Europe.*

Above left: *The climbing plants include a number which are most useful to man for their fruit, the grape, melon and cucumber for instance. This illustration, taken from* Pomona Brittanica, *published by G. Brookshaw in 1812, shows a slice cut from a melon, Cucumis. There are many varieties of fruits of this kind which have long been cultivated and improved from the wild.*

Far left: Pyrostegia venusta, *a native of Brazil and a member of a vigorous family of sun-loving climbing shrubs mainly from South and Central America up as far as Mexico. The cluster of vivid red blooms contrasts effectively with the blue of the Brazilian sky.*

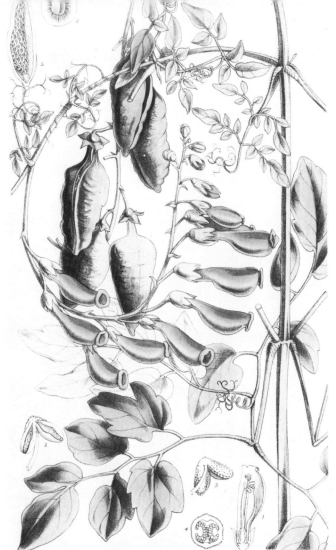

the nature of the means by which it climbs, which varies from plant to plant.

The young stem which does not find support must eventually rest its free end upon the ground. With the purchase it obtains from this, it starts off again rising upwards, while the first part of the stem remains close to the ground but usually slightly arched above it. If the second try brings it near a support, well and good, but if it does not the process is repeated. If it never finds something by which it can climb, then it perforce becomes a plant with a prostrate way of life. Climbers in this situation seldom flourish as well as those which are able to climb.

If the plant is not a woody perennial, it will die down with the season, and its destiny as a climber will have been missed for ever. There are, however, many plants which give themselves a second chance by, as it were, 'hoisting themselves up by their own bootstraps'. In these, the old growth of the previous season, which may quite well be dead, remains as a low support by which the new shoots made each year can rise. As time goes on the plant is able, in this way, to furnish its own support, each year's growth arching higher over the old growth. Such plants

rigging of a sailing ship, it should be said at once that many tropical climbers have most beautiful flowers. These may hang in graceful pendants, stand out boldly as individual blooms, or be scattered over the green curtain like a pattern. Some climbers also produce colourful and decorative fruits, and a number have highly distinctive and attractive foliage. These virtues have not escaped the attentions of the tropical gardener, who has many worthwhile climbing plants from which to choose to decorate the surroundings of his house. A leading book on tropical planting and gardening lists nearly a hundred species which can be used in this way. Readers of fiction who do ·not live in the tropics are likely to be familiar with the name of at least one of them, even though they may not have seen the plant – the colourful bougainvillea trails its decorative bracts through almost every love story and must share pride of place with the hibiscus as the plant most frequently mentioned to evoke the exotic tropical scene!

The luxuriance and variety of tropical climbers tend to distract attention from those which grow in the cooler parts of the world, but these are by no means negligible, as those who garden in temperate climes and use them to decorate their gardens and houses are well aware. The number of species of climbers native to the less warm areas is, however, much less than in the tropics, and they are absent altogether from the treeless regions of the steppes, the mountain heights and the Arctic wastes.

When climbing plants first germinate, and thrust their infant stems up through the soil, there is nothing to differentiate them from other plants. Although they stand upright and unsupported in this early stage, the growing tip of the stem very soon begins to search around for support. The subsequent behaviour of the plant depends upon two things, first, whether it finds the support it seeks and, second, if it does,

Above left: *This plant,* Eccremocarpus scaber, *was already an old-established favourite when this picture was produced for* Curtis's Botanical Magazine *in 1879. It has special interest because the motions of its stems, leaves and tendrils were described by Charles Darwin in* On the Movements and Habits of Climbing Plants. *He found that all these parts revolved and thus contributed effort towards finding support for the plant.* **Above:** *The* Minorca Honeysuckle, Lonicera implexa, *which makes up for a lack of showiness by its scent. The illustration, by Sydenham Edwards, comes from* Curtis's Botanical Magazine *of 1803.*

81

Left: *Engraving from* The Natural History of Plants *by Anton Kerner von Marilaun showing vigorous* Ficus *climbers borrowing the support of other trees and smothering them with a lattice of climbing roots, so that only the upper part of the original tree can be seen.*

Climbing plants, with their graceful habit and often lovely flowers, have not infrequently inspired men to poetry, though Thomas Tusser had his thoughts on something much less poetic when he wrote:

'The hop for his profit I thus do exalt

It strengtheneth drink and it flavoureth malt!'

A later poet, similarly inspired, capped this with:

'More graceful the hop than the far-famed vine –

More tenderly, too, doth its tendrils twine.'

But just after Thomas Tusser's time a true poetic voice began to sing. The climbing plants of the English woodland were Shakespeare's subjects:

'Sleep then, and I will wind thee in my arms

Fairies be gone, and be all ways away,

So doth the woodbine the sweet honeysuckle

Gently entwist: the female ivy so

Enrings the barky fingers of the elm.'

In a more sombre mood a modern poet of the American deep south, Beatrice Ravenal, wrote of climbers that they were:

'A splendid, strangling shroud of threaded leaves,

Strong savage tangles, succulent and wild,

Close vampire vines, the scavengers of death. . . . '

often grow into a formidable hedge-like thicket without having had recourse to anything but their own efforts.

In the great majority of cases, of course, the plant does not have to fend for itself in this way. As the seedling stem lengthens and the tip begins to move round, it comes up against some adjacent object and its climbing mechanism is brought into play. Some plants climb by twining their stems around vertical or near-vertical supports, some scramble over others by means of hooklike prickles or similar devices, others use roots to hold on to an upright surface, and yet others develop special sensitive climbing organs called tendrils which, in some cases, are provided with suckerlike discs to strengthen their hold.

The beanstalk up which Jack climbed was doubtless exactly like any other stalk of the runner bean and therefore belonged to the first category, that of the twining plants. The movement of the tip of the young stem in such plants may be clockwise or anticlockwise, but is always the same for the same species. It is not affected by light, warmth or moisture but is related to gravity. If a plant which has twined round a vertical support is turned upside down, the last two or three coils unwind and straighten, then the tip turns upwards and begins to wind round again the same way as before, though of course, because the plant is inverted, the twist is actually taking the opposite direction from the original way.

The ploy of falling over, so that it can start again from a new point if it is not at first successful in finding a support may be repeated a number of times before the plant is able to climb. It is not uncommon to see a bush or tree smothered with the growth of a climber which is rooted quite a distance away. Such situations give the impression that climbing plants are able to seek out suitable supports and can sense from a distance in which direction such a support is to be found. Our ancestors firmly believed that such was the case: in fact, however, the meeting of twining stem and support is purely fortuitous.

Some twining plants resort to another expedient if the rotating tip of the shoot is not immediately successful in its quest for support. The older portions of the stem stiffen and twist so that they attain greater rigidity. While this does not give the plant a great lift, it may be just sufficient for the free end, still rotating, to catch upon some support it would otherwise have missed. Some other plants, of which the hop is a good example, send up several stems near together if the first is not successful. These twist round one another and achieve some

Above: *This plant, a* Tropaeolum, *excited great interest when introduced by William Lobb, collector for the Victorian nurseryman, Veitch of Exeter, because the flowers were blue, whereas all the other Tropaeolums were red. The picture, by W. H. Fitch, appeared in* Curtis's Botanical Magazine.

Right: Smilax herbacea, *as this plant was called when its picture appeared in* Curtis's Botanical Magazine, *is of no particular use or beauty, unlike others illustrated, and may therefore serve to represent that army of undistinguished plants lacking ornamental or economic merit which make up the great bulk of climbers.*

semblance of rigidity which again gives the plant just that extra reach it requires.

Plants of the temperate zone with twining stems usually die down each year, although this is not invariably the case – the honeysuckles, for example, persist from year to year. In the tropical regions, however, such plants are much more common and here they give rise to those strange forms which resemble ships's ropes, one or more lianas being tightly twisted around another and stretching from the forest floor to high branches and even to the canopy.

Twining plants, by the vigour of their growth and its constricting effect on the support, may so weaken the plant which fulfils this function that it dies. Where this happens and the plant rots away, the coiled spiral of the climber remains in curious isolation, preserving in its shape, until it, too, dies, the form of its original aid. A similar effect is achieved by some plants which, although not twining climbers, behave to some extent in the same way. Some of these form lattices of branches which grow into one another and achieve the height they need by growing against rock faces, supporting their weight partly themselves and partly by leaning against the rock. In tropical countries, certain of these lattice plants grow up around trees, throwing out numerous branches and aerial roots which grow into one another forming a kind of cage completely surrounding the trunk of the tree, only the upper part of which can be seen. There is, of course, a reverse side to this coin. If a young twining plant chooses to grow up a young and vigorous tree, it may find itself as the trunk expands unable to adapt to the pressure and burst asunder. Twining climbers are for this reason rarely seen, even in tropical forests, on the trunks of the oldest and thickest trees.

The second group of climbers, those which use hooked shoots, thorns, hairs or prickles to catch hold of other plants and support themselves are perhaps better called scramblers rather than climbers. The hooks, and other aids, may be on almost any part of the stem or leaf, including the midribs and edges of the leaves. Among these plants are some very familiar to dwellers in the temperate zone, roses and blackberries both falling in this category. Almost everybody must have had experience of the efficiency of the thorns and prickles of these plants which catch hold of the clothes of the passer-by in the most aggravating fashion! It does not need any imagination to judge how apt this equipment is to hold on to other plants. The modest apparatus of the roses and blackberries, however, cannot compare with the savage spines and thorns of many tropical plants of the same kind. One writer has called these plants 'weaving' climbers, since they grow up through the thickest vegetation, not being confined to upright or semi-upright supports as the twining plants are, but weaving their way through, hooking on to anything that will give them a hold and very soon penetrating to the top of the tree where they often throw out long arching shoots and even attach themselves to adjacent trees.

Left: One of the climbers of the large genus Aristolochia *photographed in the Palm House at Kew. The inflated flowers of this plant always excite attention, in spite of their dull spotted purple-brown colouring, because of their bizarre shape. The family to which the plant belongs came to be known as the Birthworts, from the supposed effect of the plant in easing the pangs of childbirth.*

Opposite: Illustration from Buchoz' Histoire Universelle du Regne Vegetal *published in Paris in 1773 showing a climber named on the picture* Bauhinia scandens. *The contorted convultions assumed by such plants in their efforts to secure a hold on the support to enable them to climb have been well displayed by the artist in the bottom half of the picture.*

Pl. IV.

Decad. 6.

Bauhinia scandens. linn.
Folium linguæ Rumph.
6. p. 3. T. 1.
La Bauhin grimpante

a

This type of climber is seen to perfection in the climbing palms or rotangs of the tropics. The stem of these plants, if it does not immediately find a host on which to climb, loops over the ground in snakelike coils until it does, when it pushes its thin pointed leaves up through the foliage, each equipped with the most efficient anchoring barbs which find support for the thin stem as it climbs to the top of the tree. Not satisfied with this achievement, the rotang will continue to grow, looping over on to the crown of the next tree, and so on, until it reaches quite incredible lengths. Specimens have been known to reach lengths in the region of six hundred feet, and these are almost certainly not the longest.

The third type of climber is the plant which develops additional roots, not for the purpose of nutrition, but solely in order to attach itself to a vertical or upright sloping surface, up which, attaching itself by further roots as it grows, the plant climbs. The functions of these climbing roots do not usually include nutrition; they can be cut without killing the plant, though cutting the others will destroy it.

Climbing roots may be borne along the stem, as in the ivy, in which case they often become detached from the support as the stem enlarges and grows older, remaining as a mere fringe while the younger roots further up the stem take over the task of anchorage. In other cases the bunches of climbing roots are restricted to some particular point on the stem. In some plants which grow in the Himalayas small climbing roots first attach the stem to its support, but, as the plant gains vigour, stronger roots encircle the support and form beltlike clamps around it, leafy branches developing from the stem and standing out from the host tree. The climbing figs of the same area form masses of flattened roots against their supports and send aerial roots down to the ground from some way up the tree, their branches and roots being so intermixed with the host that it is difficult to distinguish between them. The host tree is often so incommoded that it cannot keep up the unequal struggle and dies, leaving the climber propped up by its aerial roots. Sir Joseph Hooker commented on the bizarre appearance of these in the journal of his famous collecting trip to the Himalayas in the middle of the last century, saying that he had seen great climbing trees 'twisting around the trunks of others and strangling them'. 'The latter', he said, 'gradually decay, leaving the sheath of climbers as one of the most remarkable of the vegetable phenomena of these mountains.' The botanist Martius, who saw similar things in the tropics where not only the host had died but the climber also, fancied that the grotesque skeletons of the latter resembled 'fantastic spectres and giant voracious monsters'!

Root climbers resemble very much plants which adopt a prostrate way of growth. The latter creep along the surface of the soil sending out bunches of roots at intervals in very much the same way as the climber ascends a wall or tree trunk. Indeed, plants like the ivy, if they cannot find some object to ascend, creep over the ground as prostrate plants, and are therefore often used by gardeners anxious to provide ground

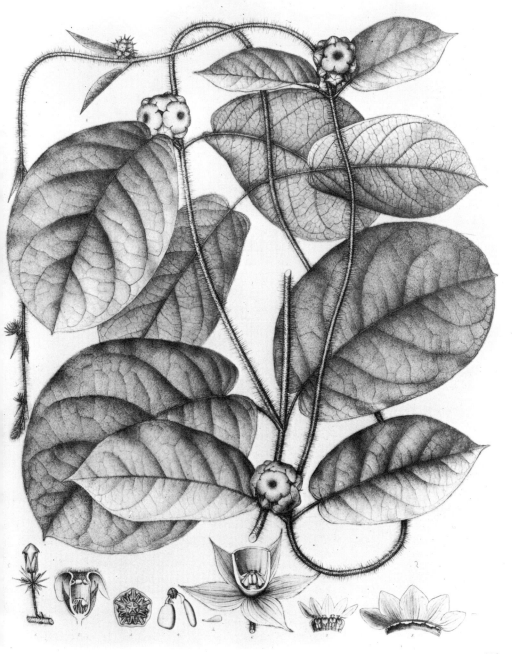

It is not generally known by those who use vanilla in cooking or consume it in flavouring that it is derived from a climbing plant – and an orchid at that! The Vanilla orchid is, in fact, the only member of the orchid family that is of economic value. There are several species, the flavouring being derived from the fermented and dried pods, the attractive taste of which was first discovered by the American Indians. Most of the vanilla of commerce comes from a species native to Mexico.

Opposite left: A charming climbing plant from the Flore des Antilles *by F. R. de Tussac, named* Alstroemeria edulis *on the illustration.*
Opposite right: The large yellow flowers of the climber shown in this photograph, Allamanda cathartica, *are a familiar sight in the tropical glasshouses of Kew Gardens, where the plant grows very well and flowers prolifically.* Allamanda *species are natives of South America. They have a great liking for strong light.*
Left: This illustration of a climbing plant named on the picture Macroscepis urceolata *is taken from* Flora Columbiae Specimina Selecta, *published by H. Karsten in Berlin in 1859.*

cover in those difficult shady areas under trees. In many root climbing plants, the way of growth alters when the need to climb lessens, the plant having reached the light and air for which it was striving. Strong stems and leaves are then thrown up into the sunshine, and this part of the plant appears quite different from the climbing portion below, where the tip of the growing stem always seems to seek the dark near the support rather than the light.

The fourth group of climbing plants includes those which have developed special sensitive organs to help them to climb. These organs, known as tendrils, will be well known to most people because that common vegetable the pea uses this method of climbing. They stand out straight at first but curl round any body with which they come into contact. Tendrils may be formed either from leaves or from stems – or even roots! Their origin is sometimes clearly indicated by the way they arise, but there are many cases where their precise nature is doubtful. Before they make contact the tips show a regular rotating movement and when young are very sensitive to touch, bending within a matter of minutes towards the direction of the side on which they were touched. As soon as the tip obtains a hold, the rest of the tendril contracts into a spiral, so that the main body of the plant is brought nearer the support. The spiralling turns the tendril into a spring which is able to absorb the force of the wind on the plant which, if the tendril remained rigid, might be broken away.

Tendrils are produced in considerable numbers. As soon as a stem has anchored itself by one, another grasps a support in a different direction and as it moves upwards the plant is firmly anchored at many points. At the top of the host fresh shoots arise and arch over, throwing out tendrils in their turn which may grasp a branch of an adjacent host. The two hosts are thus linked by a bridge to which other stems attach themselves, thus forming pendulous masses of vegetation. Tendrils give the climbing plant which possesses them an adaptability and efficiency in climbing which exceeds that of plants using any other method. This, no doubt, is the reason why more plants use this method than the others.

If ease in attaining their object is the criterion by which the success of plants is to be judged, climbers are very much more adept than other plants. The giant trees which form the canopy of the tropical forest carry on their activities in the main at the top, where they have succeeded in reaching the sunshine. The main bulk of the tree, whose sole purpose is to hold the remainder up in the air and light, is, in a sense, wasted tissue weighing many tons which has been raised only by laborious effort over many years. Yet among the canopy, overtopping it and stealing the light from it, are the climbers, which have expended only a fraction of the time and effort which has been put out by the tree in getting their flowers and leaves in precisely the same favourable position as those of the tree itself! The climbers are clearly the opportunists of the vegetable world and, as in human life, they generally succeed in carrying off the greatest share of what is to be won!

Below: The familiar Cat's Tail or Timothy Grass, Phleum pratense, *from* Icones et Descriptiones Graminum Austriacorum *by N. T. Host, published in Vienna in 1801. This is one of the most common and valuable grasses of British meadows and pastures. Its leaves are comparatively broad and have rough edges, so that animals find it rather harsh and coarse when it is growing and do not relish it. It does, however, yield heavy crops of very good hay.*

Below right: The tall tassels of a flowering plant of the sugar-cane family, Saccharum, *blowing in the wind in the warm climate of Nigeria. Sugar-cane, which has been cultivated in many countries for a long time, is by far the most important member of this genus, but some other members are ornamental in appearance.*

All Flesh is Grass

'The bare earth, till then
Desert and bare, unsightly, unadorned,
Brought forth the tender grass, whose verdure clad
Her universal face with pleasant green. . . .'
John Milton

That master of paradox, G. K. Chesterton, centred one of his stories about the priest-detective Father Brown around the point that some things are so familiar to us that although we see them our consciousness does not record any impact from them. In his story everyone saw the murderer, who happened to be the postman, but, when questioned about what happened at the scene of the crime, failed to mention that the postman had called, simply because this was part of the normal routine and was unconsciously dismissed from the mind. Those of us who live in temperate lands are in very much the same position with regard to grasses. We are so familiar with them and they are so much part of our background that they go unregarded except by farmers and those with a special interest. Moreover, most people know nothing about them, except that it is hard work mowing the lawn!

If you want to give yourself a simple test on your knowledge of grasses, ask yourself whether you can recollect having seen a grass flower and, if so, what the flower looks like. Can you say, even, whether the grass is a flowering plant or not? And yet,

you see grass every day, even those of you who live in the big cities, and thousands upon thousands of grass plants grow in your garden, in the park, on the golf course, or wherever you walk. The answer is, of course, that the grasses are flowering plants. You will almost certainly have seen the flowers, but since they are not the gaudy, highly coloured and often highly perfumed productions to which we mostly apply the name of flower, being small and generally insignificant, you may be excused for not having recognised them!

Bamboos are a kind of grass. The flowers of both bamboos and grasses are borne in what the botanists call 'spikelets', each of which, inside some chaffy scales called 'glumes', carries one or more tiny flowers. A number of spikelets makes up the inflorescence. Each spikelet is protected by a bristle called an awn, and within are the stamens and stigmas, the latter being situated on the ovary. The stamens are hairlike and quiver at the slightest breeze, so that the pollen is readily shaken from them by the wind, the grasses being, as hay-fever sufferers know, wind pollinated. Some observers have claimed that grasses have regular times of the day for opening their flowers and that this varies from plant to plant.

Although the flowers of grasses are small, lack colour and are therefore not very noticeable, there are a number of them whose graceful and attractive inflorescences have earned them a place in the garden. One very commonly grown in northern temperate gardens is the Pampas Grass, which is much in demand when dried for floral arrangements. Many bamboos find a place in gardens, partly for their graceful way of growth and partly because they form an effective screen. Bamboos are not grown for their flowers, as they take many years to reach the flowering stage and die immediately afterwards.

The leaves of grasses are, with a few exceptions, thin, long and pointed. They sheathe the stem, which is hollow, unlike the plants of the sedge family, often mistaken for grasses, which have solid stems and leaves that completely surround the stem like a tube. The great majority of grasses are herbs and do not make woody tissue, the exception being the giant bamboos. They vary enormously in size, the smallest herbaceous species being less than an inch in height, while the great grasses of the

As man has not yet discovered an easy method of converting harvested grass directly into palatable food for himself, the most economical way he can use grass at present is to allow animals which can digest grass to eat it and then eat the animals, obtaining the benefits of the grass feed at second-hand. Three quarters of the world's feeding grassland is used as grazing in this way. Much of the rest is used as hay, the making of which is a rather more skilled process than those not involved might think. The ideal is to dehydrate the mown grass to a moisture content of 15 per cent or less, but this is often quite difficult to achieve. The crop must be harvested well before the grass reaches maturity so as to obtain the highest protein content, but, cut too early, pasture may be damaged and future yield decreased. And then there is always the weather: rain at the wrong time can reduce a crop by as much as half. There are modern ways of overcoming these difficulties but they are expensive.

Above: A small tufted grass named on the illustration, which is taken from Host's Graminum Austriacorum, *as* Sesleria echinata.

Below right*: Seed heads of* Sorghum, *photographed in Mauritania. Sorghum is a maize-like grass which has been cultivated since early times for food purposes and is the leading cereal grain in Africa, being important also in a number of other countries. The grain is higher in protein and lower in fat than maize. Sorghum is very resistant to heat and drought, replacing maize in hot, dry regions.*

tropical savannahs range up to nearly twenty feet. These are dwarfed, however, by the giant bamboos of Asia which may exceed a hundred feet!

The upright stems of the grasses are called 'culms'. They are usually conspicuously jointed, the joints being solid, not hollow like the remainder of the stem. The stems are smooth and polished, the skin cells containing a considerable amount of silica, which is left as a white skeleton if the grass is burnt. Many tropical grasses have numerous branches, this being a characteristic of the bamboos in particular. Some of the tropical species are climbers, growing to a length of two hundred feet. Grass culms grow very rapidly, bamboos occasionally growing as much as twenty-five feet in a month, at times at a rate of two to three feet per hour!

Many of the perennial grasses spread by creeping stems underground, others by stems that creep along horizontally above the ground. They give off branches at every joint and thus possess a powerful and rapid means of covering the ground. Grasses have fibrous roots and develop a very extensive rooting system. It is an amazing fact that in some cases the roots of a

Above: *Illustration of a grass he called* Rotboellia incurvata *taken from Host's* Graminum Austriacorum. *George Nicholson, the Curator of Kew at the end of the last century who compiled* The Illustrated Dictionary of Gardening, *wrote of the members of the genus* Rotboellia *that 'they are more curious than beautiful.'*

Above right: *Rice*, Oryza sativa, *growing at Jaffra in Sri Lanka.*

Right and opposite left: *Graceful portraits of two members of the genus* Holcus *as named and depicted in Host's* Graminum Austriacorum *showing the delicate and lovely spikes and, in the smaller* drawings, *the individual grass flowers.*

Opposite above right: Chloris distichophylla, *a decorative and graceful grass photographed in the wild at Imbancu in Brazil in the course of a Kew expedition in 1965.*

Opposite below right: *One of the Pampas Grasses,* Cortaderia sellowana, *photographed on Comprida Islands in Brazil in the course of the same Kew expedition in 1965. The Pampas Grasses have great ornamental value and stand up so grandly and statuesquely when in flower that they are often used as a central feature in lawns or other garden designs.*

single grass plant, if they were stretched out end to end, would reach a length of several miles!

The grasses are the most widely distributed of all flowering plants, an estimated 30 per cent of the earth's land vegetation being dominated by grasses. Several other families contain larger numbers of species, but no other family can equal the grasses in the number of individual plants. The largest grass-dominated areas are the steppes of Asia and the plains and prairies of North America, but every continent has its share of such regions, although in many cases the grasses are mixed with trees and shrubs. The bamboos form extensive forest areas in tropical and sub-tropical lands. The gracefulness of these plants as they sway in the wind is very pleasing – except to the traveller who wishes to pass through them, since they are often virtually impenetrable!

The savannahs of the tropics contain the largest number of different kinds of grasses, though grasses do not form such a large part of the plant population in the tropics as they do in the cooler lands. The further from the equator, the higher the proportion of grasses in the total plant population, and in Arctic and Antarctic regions grasses comprise a quarter of the vegetation. Grasses are also the most numerous plants in the high mountains and are usually dominant above the timber line for as far as vegetation can be found. They find it possible to

Holcus lanatus

live on sand dunes and in salt marshes where for other plants life is intolerable and also populate arid regions where other vegetation is sparse. Grasses almost always prefer the sunlight to shade, but a few species may be found in the forest undergrowth in the tropics. There are also a few woodland grasses in the temperate regions, but these are a tiny proportion only of the whole.

The fruit of the grasses is small, ovoid and rounded, with a furrow along one side, and is usually referred to as a grain, a name which gives the key to the most important fact about the grass family: it contains those grain-producing species which provide man and his livestock with the major part of their food supply – and, since these species are involved in the production of beer, whisky, rum and other alcoholic beverages, his drink also! The cereals wheat, barley, oats and rye are grasses; so are the plants which serve the same purpose in tropical or subtropical countries – rice, maize, sorghum and other millets; and so is the Sugar Cane. All these are the source of a number of manufactured products as well as food, including such unlikely things as paper, plastics and cosmetics.

From the grasslands, whether natural or sown by man, our grazing animals derive food, either by eating it green as it stands or stored as hay, silage or in some manufactured form. From these animals come dairy products and the meat we eat. The grasses are of incalculable value to man, since it is largely

Opposite left: A grass named on the picture as Andropogon ravennae, *again from Host's book. The illustration brings out very well the graceful arching leaves and the feathery spike of this species, whose ornamental qualities are high.*
Opposite right: The Building Bamboo of Java, Gigantochloa verticillata, *in the Palm House at Kew. Young shoots of this grow from ground level to the top of the Palm House in one season, a height of over 60 feet. It resembles, and is little smaller than, the Giant Bamboo of Burma. In spite of its size, it is a graceful species. As its name implies, it is of considerable use in the construction industry in its native country.*

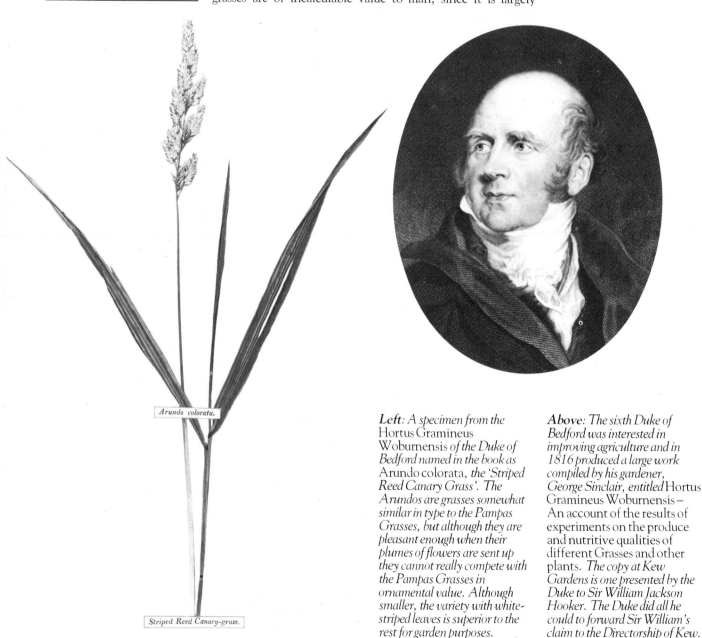

Arundo colorata.

Striped Reed Canary-grass.

Left: *A specimen from the* Hortus Gramineus Woburnensis *of the Duke of Bedford named in the book as* Arundo colorata, *the 'Striped Reed Canary Grass'. The Arundos are grasses somewhat similar in type to the Pampas Grasses, but although they are pleasant enough when their plumes of flowers are sent up they cannot really compete with the Pampas Grasses in ornamental value. Although smaller, the variety with white-striped leaves is superior to the rest for garden purposes.*

Above: *The sixth Duke of Bedford was interested in improving agriculture and in 1816 produced a large work compiled by his gardener, George Sinclair, entitled* Hortus Gramineus Woburnensis – An account of the results of experiments on the produce and nutritive qualities of different Grasses and other plants. *The copy at Kew Gardens is one presented by the Duke to Sir William Jackson Hooker. The Duke did all he could to forward Sir William's claim to the Directorship of Kew.*

through them that the energy captured by plants from sunlight in photosythesis is made available to us, the contribution from all other plant families taken together being less than that of the grasses.

Although the bamboos supply some food, notably the young shoots, their main contribution arises from the hardness of their wood and its ability to split easily. This makes them immensely useful in the construction industry in the countries where they are common and in the production of furniture and a great variety of household and other goods, including even hats, clothing and umbrellas! The number of uses to which bamboos and their products are put in these countries is immense.

One use of grasses derives from their property of making a sward. Far more than other plants they can stand frequent and close cutting which is of great use in the creation of lawns for pleasure and recreation, on aerodromes or anywhere else where a close cut carpet-like surface is required. Without grasses, the ball games of high skill such as cricket and bowls, which depend entirely upon a close-mown grass surface for their proper performance, would never have come into existence, and the lives of all those people who enjoy these games would have been that much poorer.

Another virtue of the grasses turned to good use by man arises from their extensive root system, the capacity of many species

Andropogon Ravennae

Elymus crinitus

Left: A grass from Host's work named Elymus crinitus *on the illustration. Grasses of the genus* Elymus *are natives of the north temperate region. Although they are not ornamental, the one species native to Great Britain,* Elymus arenarius, *the Sea Lymegrass, is of considerable use. It grows in abundance on some shores, forming large bluish-green patches. The long creeping roots are able to bind the sand so that, under its protection, other plants can gain a hold.*

Right: An attractive plate of the Sugar-Cane from Tussac's Flore des Antilles. *This has always been one of the world's most important crops, and the possession of the 'Sugar Islands' in the West Indies was a considerable factor in the wars fought between Great Britain and France in the eighteenth century.*

to spread rapidly by creeping stems and their tolerance of harsh conditions. The mass of fibrous roots which they make is very effective in holding loose soil together. If, therefore, they can be made to grow on the edge of an area of soil erosion they will prevent it spreading further and, properly managed, can initiate the process of reclamation. Grasses are being used to immense effect in this way in countries such as Holland. In contrast, of course, if areas of the world where grasses grow naturally are deprived of their grass blanket the retaining element of the soil will be lost and soil erosion will almost certainly set in. The classic case of this in the western world was the ploughing up of the plains of North America; the resulting loss of grass eventually resulted in the 'dust bowl' conditions of the 1930s, the human misery of which was so effectively described by John Steinbeck in his novel *The Grapes of Wrath*. There are many areas in other parts of the world where similar havoc has been created by unwise farming practices.

Inconspicuous though many of them are, the grasses are of such importance to man that, if they had not existed, he would have found his Biblical mandate to 'increase and multiply' very much harder to fulfill in the colder northern countries. The food grains, protected from predators, enabled him to set by a store of food for the winter in these countries where, unlike the tropics, nature goes into a state of suspended animation in that season and food is hard to find. Among the plants, grasses qualify more than any others to be called the friend of man.

Above: *At work in the rice fields. The importance of rice as a food crop in the Eastern countries cannot be over-estimated, and it is the staple food of the native population of tropical Asia. The plant is indigenous to that area and has been cultivated there since the earliest times. Its grain furnishes a larger proportion of the food of the human race than does any other plant.*

Below: *A thickly-tufted grass from Host's work named on the picture as* Heleochloa schoenoides.

Mountain Fire

Between the teeming plains of India and the high and sparsely populated lands of Tibet lie the vast ranges of the Himalayan mountains. Folded and faulted in ancient times on a scale greater than the imagination can easily compass, studded with great peaks that reach up in awful loneliness through the barren snows, pierced by mighty rivers flowing through incredible gorges, this enormous land mass provides every variety of climate and plant habitat.

The full force of the monsoon from the Bay of Bengal drives up against the eastern Himalayas. Yearly average rainfalls of fifty to eighty inches are normal for the southward-facing slopes, and some places have totals much greater. In this region rain-forest at the lowest levels gives way above three thousand feet to a cooler type of forest vegetation, and magnolias and rhododendrons become common above six thousand feet. Still higher, the magnolias thin out and the conifers increase, but before the trees begin to degenerate into scrub rhododendrons become dominant. This is, indeed, the land of the rhododendron. Here is its natural home and centre. An area from northern Tibet through northern Burma and extending into southern China and Tibet contains something like three quarters of the known species.

The average temperature of the Himalayas at seven thousand feet in summer is 65 degrees Farenheit (18 degrees Centigrade) and in the winter 44 degrees Fahrenheit (7 degrees Centigrade). Plants which grow at that elevation or above do not, therefore, find conditions in the moister parts of the temperate zone too dissimilar, particularly in coastal or island situations where the range of temperature is subject to the moderating influence of the sea and the rainfall is higher than inland. These areas of the Himalayas are thus a very fruitful source of garden plants for the temperate zone, and the rhododendrons which form such a prominent part of the plant population there are not the least among the groups to have contributed to the enrichment of the gardens of that zone.

Rhododendrons vary enormously in size, from large trees to tiny plants which hug the ground. Frank Kingdon-Ward, who made many plant-collecting expeditions to this region in the 1920s and 1930s, described a rhododendron which he saw on the Burma Tibet frontier in 1931. It was fifty feet high and the trunk was nearly six feet in girth towards the base. It was in full bloom, bearing over eight hundred trusses of flowers, each truss with twenty-five to thirty large bell-like blossoms, rose-purple in colour – an unforgettable sight as it flamed in the evening sun.

In the thickest forest, where plants are drawn up by their neighbours, greater heights than that of this tree may be attained, some specimens rising as high as eighty feet. Thousands of square miles of forest hanging upon the lower slopes of the Himalayas are full of such rhododendrons. It is not, indeed, uncommon for large areas to be wholly dominated by rhododendron trees. Most of them are, of course, smaller than the giant which Kingdon-Ward saw and, where the forest thins out, many of them are shrubs rather than trees, often forming almost impenetrable thickets.

Those who have seen the Asiatic rhododendron only in the gardens and on the estates of the western world can have but a limited notion of what it is like in its native habitat. Cloud, mist and rain are the daily portion of those areas where it grows, but when the weather clears and the sun breaks through on to the steep vegetation-covered slopes running down to the torrent in the valley, crossed by a shaky rope bridge, with the snow-covered peaks towering up an unbelievable distance into the clear blue above, the bright colours of the flowers are picked out and the whole scene takes on an unbelievable beauty and majesty.

As the forest thins out into scrub country, along the sides of the valleys, in niches in the rocks, hanging over dripping water, in any secluded nook or patch which provides a foothold, are to be found the smaller rhododendrons. Many of them are most attractive shrubs and possess the added virtue that, when brought from their native home and grown in gardens, they are of a much more manageable size than the trees of the forest. The very smallest of them grow in places above the scrub or where, in other regions, heaths would usually be found. They behave, indeed, very much like heaths, forming large mats, sometimes acres in extent, covered in the spring with many thousands of blooms. They are often so thickly interlaced that it is possible to walk on them.

On one expedition Frank Kingdon-Ward crossed the valley

Opposite: Rhododendron griffithianum *drawn by W. H. Fitch. This is one of the finest rhododendrons and parent of some magnificent hybrids.*
Above: Rhododendron luteum *in the Zigana pass, Turkey. This is a long-standing garden favourite which flowers well and has a lovely fragrance.*

Below: Rhododendron lacteum, *a beautiful species introduced by George Forrest in 1910 from Yunnan, where it was growing at 12,000 feet.*
Right: Rhododendron linearifolium, *a curious garden form of a Japanese species, distinguished by its shaggy hairiness, narrow leaves and long thin petals.*

Right: An artist's glamorous impression of the young Joseph Hooker receiving plants from collectors. Though this is an idealised picture, the original drawing from which it was made being much more like the real thing, it still conveys the essential point that a successful expedition of the kind made by Sir Joseph into the Himalayas depended entirely on enlisting the services of the local population to help in searching for plants.

Below: Rhododendron pendulum, *one of the rhododendrons collected by Sir Joseph Hooker on his expedition into Sikkim and included in the book published by his father before Joseph returned from India. The book was illustrated by coloured lithographs, prepared by W. H. Fitch from Joseph's drawings, and was published under the title of* Rhododendrons of the Sikkim-Himalaya. *The pure white flowers of* Rhododendron pendulum *are small compared with those of others introduced by Sir Joseph, and the shrub itself is not large, being an epiphyte on trees. It tends to hang down, the leaves and flowers being borne towards the ends of the stems, which are three to four feet long.*

of one the great rivers, the Tsang-po, which, lower down its course, becomes the Brahmaputra. The gorges by which the Tsang-po breaks through the vast Himalayan barrier from Tibet are one of the wonders of the world. On this occasion he was trying to make his way among them towards a pass around the great mountain of Namcha Barwa. As he climbed up to it the weather deteriorated, but through the mist and showers he could see that his effort might have an unexpected reward. 'If the weather was discomforting,' he writes excitedly, 'the scene which revealed itself to me' compensated for the unpleasantness – 'the valley was alight with flowers. Rhododendrons, dwarf in stature, yet hoary with age, sprawled and writhed in every direction. . . . The whole rock floor was hotly carpeted, and over the cliffs poured an incandescent stream of living lava!' There were twenty-five different species of rhododendron in that valley, 'more than half of which had never before been noticed by man'.

The flowers of rhododendrons are among the showiest to be found in the whole of the plant kingdom. This is in part because of their habit of bearing their flowers not singly but in trusses, the natural massing together contributing greatly to their spectacular aspect. The individual flowers are often, however, of great beauty, both in colour and delicate markings, particularly on the throat. In some kinds the petals have a waxy appearance which adds to their attractiveness. Colours vary

from white through all shades of pink, red and scarlet to mauve and purple, including what might be called 'near blue'. A definite and positive blue does not seem to exist among the wild plants, although it has been achieved among the hybrids bred from them.

The leaves of rhododendrons are also attractive and add greatly to the ornamental value of the plants, many of the middle range of the family being neat bushes thickly furnished with trim dark green foliage, rendering them very suitable for use as free standing specimens in gardens. The leaves of the dwarf alpine kinds are very small, though the largest grow nearly three feet long and a foot wide. The undersides of the leaves of some of the larger species are furnished with a felt-like covering of tan, brown or silver, which also extends to the young shoots and gives the whole bush a most elegant appearance.

Rhododendrons form a mass of fibrous roots near the surface and when grown in gardens do best when they do not have to compete with shallow rooting trees. They are happiest with oaks, which seek their moisture and nutriment lower down. Their shallow rooting habit makes it easy to move them but

Above: A magnificent rhododendron reproduced from Rhododendrons of the Sikkim-Himalaya *called on the illustration* Rhododendron argenteum *but regarded as* Rhododendron grande. *The leaves have a distinctive and most attractive silvery underside. There are twenty-five or so flowers in each truss, individual blossoms being ivory-white blotched at the base. This species makes a large shrub or small tree thirty feet high.*

Left: A chalk portrait by George Richmond of Sir Joseph Hooker as a young man of thirty-eight. Sir Joseph was not very pleased with it, as he thought it made him look 'a very lackadaisical young gentleman'!

brings with it the disadvantage that they easily suffer from drought. When the top layer of soil dries out they are unable to obtain water even though it may not be too far away lower down. In their native home in areas of high rainfall such conditions rarely arise. When they do, the rhododendron population suffers severely. Both Kingdon-Ward and George Forrest, another famous plant collector, saw such damage over many miles of country.

Although the larger part of the rhododendron genus is found in the Himalayas, there is a substantial outlying section which has made its home further south. A number of species, possibly about a third of the number which grows in the Himalayas, is found in Malaysia, Java, New Guinea and the Philippines, one species having reached Australia. Many of these are as attractive as the best of the Himalayan rhododendrons, but, like those which come from the lower and warmer levels of the Himalayas, they are not hardy in the temperate zone and have to be grown as glasshouse plants. They are not likely, therefore, ever to become as well known as those from the Himalayas.

There are no rhododendrons in Africa or South America, but North America is the home of some of the most attractive and well-known species, including the Rhodora, the Pinkster Flower and Flame Azalea. These are not, however, of the evergreen type with which we have hitherto been concerned. They are of the kind which shed their leaves in the winter and are universally known as azaleas – although, in fact, botanically speaking they are indistinguishable from and classed as rhododendrons. When William Bartram, son of John Bartram, the famous American plant collector of the eighteenth century, first saw the Flame Azalea in 1791 he called it the 'fiery azalea, flaming on the ascending hills or wavy surface of the

Top left: *Illustration from Sir Joseph Hooker's* Himalayan Journals, *published in London in 1854, showing snow beds at 13,000 feet in the Th'lonok Valley with rhododendrons in blossom and Kinchinjunga in the distance.*

Top right: *Rhododendron wightii, reproduced from* Rhododendrons of the Sikkim-Himalaya, *a small shrubby tree six to fourteen feet high. The compact flower head contains up to twenty bell-shaped pale straw-coloured*

flowers beautifully spotted red.
Left: *A beautiful red rhododendron named Rhododendron lancifolium as depicted by W. H. Fitch.*
Opposite: *The Rhododendron Dell in Kew Gardens in spring. The Dell is an artificial hollow*

cut out by 'Capability' Brown using the Staffordshire Militia (at Kew as guard for the King) in the 1760s. Planted then with laurels, and known as the Laurel Vale, it was converted to a rhododendron walk in the nineteenth century.

gliding brooks. The epithet fiery', he said, 'I annex to this most celebrated species of azalea, as being expressive of the appearance of its flowers, which are in general of the colour of the finest red lead, orange and bright gold, as well as yellow and cream colour; these various splendid colours are not only in separate plants, but frequently all the varieties and shades are seen in separate branches on the same plant; and the clusters of the blossoms cover the shrubs in such incredible profusion on the hillsides, that suddenly opening to view from the dark shades, we are alarmed with the apprehension of the hill.being set on fire. This is certainly the most gay and brilliant flowering shrub yet known.' This is not an exaggarated account. Hybrids bred from this species are among the finest and showiest of hardy shrubs in cultivation in temperate lands.

A similar comment could equally well be applied to those species which are natives of Japan, which, like North America, possesses few species of rhododendron, but among them some with qualities which make them outstanding. The Japanese azaleas are not deciduous but evergreen like the general run of rhododendrons. Both the American and the Japanese species have been so extensively hybridised that the precise origin of those grown in gardens is uncertain. Their origin may be in doubt, but the attractiveness of the Japanese azaleas is not, nor is their usefulness. The best forms are characterised by the startling brightness of the colours of their flowers, the neatness of their habit of growth and the intense autumn colours of their leaves. Without the garden varieties bred from American and Japanese species and their hybridisation with other rhododendrons the gardens of the temperate zone would be much poorer.

A few species grow in Europe, and it was naturally one of these which was recorded as the first rhododendron to be introduced (in 1656) to western gardens. The American Swamp Honeysuckle was the next to be introduced, in 1680, but it was not until the eighteenth century that this plant

Above: *Although a comparatively small shrub, reaching only four feet in height,* Rhododendron fulgens *is an outstanding member of the genus because of the deep bright blood-red colour of its somewhat fleshy, highly polished and shining flowers, carried in dense heads. Its leaves, which are rather broad, are woolly underneath.*

Right: *The brownish-red long-tubed rather waxy flowers of this species,* Rhododendron roylii, *reproduced from* Rhododendrons of the Sikkim-Himalaya, *are quite distinct and striking. They are held in a loose head of four to eight blooms on long slender branches and contrast therefore very markedly with the compactness of the head of* R. fulgens *above.*

Opposite: Magnolia grandiflora, *shown in a plate from Buchoz'* Histoire Universelle, *is, in its native North America, a handsome stately evergreen tree forming a fine head pyramidal in shape and bearing flowers of equal dignity, some six to eight inches across, pure white and sweetly scented.*

Pl. I

Decad. 6.

Magnolia maximo flore foliis
subtus ferrugineis.
Rand hort.chelf. p. 132.
Magnolia grandiflora linn. Sp. plant.755.
Laurier Tulipier.

Cette plante est reduitte à moitié.

One of the virtues of magnolias, perhaps the most splendid of all hardy trees because of the size of their flowers, is their exceptional freedom from disease. Occasional leaf-spot or attack by wood-rot is all they seem to suffer. They do, however, present one serious difficulty in cultivation. Their roots are comparatively thick and fleshy and are easily damaged. They are apt to decay when this happens, so that it is best to move them when they are growing vigorously in May, there being a better chance then of healing possible damage than at times when the plant is resting. As they are trees or large shrubs they need a good deal of room to develop, but even a small garden can greatly enhance its attraction if a specimen is planted as a central feature. A varied collection can bring great distinction to the larger garden, and for a spring display there is nothing to equal the early-flowering types.

Opposite: *A charming picture of* Magnolia grandiflora *taken from Mark Catesby's* Natural History of Carolina, Florida and the Bahama Islands, *published in London in 1754.* **Left:** *The strikingly deep colour of the flowers of this magnolia photographed in Kew Gardens contrasts with the lighter varieties shown elsewhere and indicates the range of colour in these plants.*

became at all widely known. Even as late as the beginning of the nineteenth century no more than ten or fifteen kinds were included in the records but after the Napoleonic wars more began to be brought in, the first Himalayan rhododendron with red flowers reaching the west in 1815. It was Joseph Hooker, son of Sir William Hooker, Director of Kew, and later Director himself, who popularised the Himalayan rhododendron. He was the first of the great rhododendron collectors. His expedition to the Sikkim Himalayas in 1848 and the following years was a classic. Richly productive in specimens and seeds, it was fully chronicled and documented both botanically and popularly and was a tremendous contribution to the knowledge of a hitherto virtually unknown region.

When Hooker arrived in India the flora of the eastern Himalayas had not been examined and he had no inkling of the richness of the region in rhododendron species. His first trip in May 1848 into Sikkim territory added three, 'one scarlet, one white with superb foliage, and one the most lovely thing you can imagine; a parasite on gigantic trees, three yards high, with whorls of branches and 3–6 immense white deliciously deep-scented flowers at the apex of each branch.' He thought this one the 'most splendid thing of the kind' he had ever seen. This journey was followed by a number of others, each adding some more species of rhododendron to the total; eventually he got up into Tibet, reaching nineteen thousand feet at his highest point. Even at eighteen thousand feet, almost at this height, he was able to collect one which, for obvious reasons, he called the Snow Rhododendron. 'The hard woody branches of this curious little species, as thick as a goose quill, straggle along the ground for a foot or two, presenting brown tufts of vegetation. . . . The branches are densely interwoven [and] . . . wholly depressed: whence the shrub, spreading horizontally, and barely raised two inches above the soil, becomes eminently typical of the arid stern climate it inhabits', exposed to 'the joint influences of a scorching sun by day, and the keenest frost at night – of the greatest drought followed in a few hours by a saturated atmosphere. . . . During genial weather, when the sun heats the soil to 150°F, its perfumed foliage scents the air, while to snowstorm and frost it is insensible, blooming through all, expanding its little purple flowers to the day . . . .'

The rhododendrons that Joseph Hooker sent home from this expedition opened up a new world of which there had previously been no conception, and it is to him that credit must be given for revealing the riches of the rhododendrons of the Himalayas to the western temperate world. In his collection were included many of the finest garden and cool greenhouse species. These were immediately seized upon and used by breeders to produce a host of attractive hybrids which, in areas where rhododendrons grow well, were so lavishly planted that they greatly altered the appearance of woodland gardens.

For a considerable time after Hooker's memorable expedition little further progress was made. Although French Missionaries in China despatched many dried specimens from that area, they sent few living plants and little seed. It was not until the famous firm of Veitch of Chelsea sent out a Kew-trained collector, E. H. Wilson, at the turn of the century that Asiatic rhododendrons began to be received once again in the west. From that time onward until the Second World War a series of notable collectors worked in various parts of the region. Wilson was followed by George Forrest and Frank Kingdon-Ward, both already mentioned. Others were Reginald Farrer, Captain F. M. Baily, R. E. Cooper and the American J. F. Rock. A notable triumvirate of the thirties were Ludlow, Sherriff and George Taylor, the last afterwards becoming Director of Kew. Although some of these collectors made a number of trips to the

region and their contributions greatly augmented the number of species available to grow in western gardens, much enriching the resources which can be used for the production of hybrids, there are still vast areas, particularly in China, which have been only cursorily investigated and others which have not been entered at all. There may well be further treasures to be discovered. Unfortunately, the political situation is such that opportunities do not exist to continue the work.

A frequent companion of the Himalayan rhododendron, except in the upper reaches of its habitat, is the magnolia, another most attractive tree or shrub, quite as beautiful as the rhododendron, but in a different way. In the areas where they grow together, the magnolia and the rhododendron often dominate the scene; in other places the magnolia grows in groves or woods of its own. The magnolia has aroused interest botanically because it is among the most primitive of flowering plants and may be a progenitor of the rhododendron itself. A large number of fossils have been found, showing that the genus was formerly much more widely distributed than it is now.

Magnolias are not so centred on the Himalayas as rhododendrons. They are found in the east in a triangular region of which the three corners are the eastern Himalayas, Japan and Java, but a number are also found in America over an area from the eastern United States through Mexico and Central America to northern South America. Roughly a third of the total species is

Opposite: Seen close up, as in this photograph of a mature magnolia in full bloom in spring at Kew, there hardly seems to be a shoot on this tree which does not bear a magnificent large blossom, and there are more waiting to open.

Top: This photograph of an old specimen of Magnolia soulangiana *in full blossom at Kew shows how floriferous these*

trees can be, outdoing even Japanese cherries.

Above: Fully open flowers of Magnolia soulangiana *at Kew. This popular hybrid between* M. denudata *(the Yulan) and* M. liliflora *flowers in April, a little later than the Yulan, coming out as the flowers of the latter are fading and continuing until June, the two providing a succession of blooms for several months.*

American. They differ from the Asiatic kinds in that those which are not deciduous do not flower until after the leaves have formed, whereas the Asiatic species flower on the bare branches. About half the Asiatic magnolias are evergreen trees and shrubs of the tropics and are thus not hardy in temperate lands; a somewhat larger proportion of the American species will not tolerate such conditions.

The first magnolias to come into cultivation were those from America, one of which was brought to England in 1688. The first hardy Asiatic species did not appear in the west until 1789. Others followed until all the hardy American species were being grown. As Japan was opened up in the 1860s, four notable new ones reached America from that country, and the remarkable *Magnolia campbellii* was introduced into Britain from the Himalayas in 1868. No Chinese magnolias had yet reached the west, but the collectors E. H. Wilson and George Forrest effectively changed this. From 1900 onwards they explored south-west China and introduced a number of new kinds; these were an instant success, because their flowers are much finer than those of most of the American kinds and are seen much earlier – and, on the unclothed branches, to better advantage.

The magnolias are all either trees or shrubs with rather large leaves. Their flowers are also large, simple and showy, varying from white through pink to purple, with green to yellow also represented. The only American species which can hold its own with the Asiatics is the handsome Bull Bay, a large evergreen tree with white flowers which grows in the south-east of the United States. The showiest is *Magnolia campbellii*, which has 'shocking' pink flowers ten inches across, borne, on the mature tree, in thousands. A specimen of this tree, or of one of the hybrids bred from it, in full blossom is probably the most magnificent sight, in the plant world, that nature has to offer. Growing in numbers in its native Himalayan forests scattered or

grouped on the slopes, and seen from above to the best advantage, it is a sight to take the breath away. Its only disadvantage as a garden plant, apart from its borderline hardiness, is the length of time, twenty-five years or so, that it takes to come into flower from seed.

One of the curious facts about magnolias is the complete absence of hybrids in the wild, although the genus hybridises freely in cultivation. It is all the more strange, therefore, that the most common representative in gardens is not one of the wild species but a hybrid, *Magnolia soulangiana*, which was bred in France, near Paris, in 1820 of two Asiatic species, one of which was white and the other purple. It has many varieties which vary in colour from almost pure white to those with deep rose purple on the outside of the petals.

The magnolia and the rhododendron, bred in high places among the great peaks, companions both in the Himalayan forests and in the gardens of men, stand in the plant world in a place of their own. Equalled in beauty and presence by few other plants, they will continue, so long as man makes gardens, to bring to his creations a nobility and grandeur which raises them above the commonplace. We are, indeed, fortunate that such plants exist.

Above: A magnolia captioned on the illustration Magnolia umbrella, *but now* M. tripetala. *A native of eastern North America, it takes its name of 'Umbrella Tree' from the fancied resemblance of the cluster of leaves at the end of the shoots to an umbrella.*
Left: A flower of Magnolia liliflora, *a species from China and the parent of* M. soulangiana *which brought the purple colour into that hybrid.*
Opposite: The most magnificent of all magnolias, M. campbellii, *pictured in Sir Joseph Hooker's* Drawings of Himalayan Plants. *This large tree, as high as 150 feet in the wild, bears deep pink flowers, each up to ten inches across, in profusion.*

Plate IV

Water Misers

'And cactuses, a queen might don,
If weary of a golden crown,
And still appear as royal.'
Elizabeth Barrett Browning

In the world of science fiction, Frank Herbert, in his long and entertaining epic *Dune*, centres the struggle for control of a galactic empire around a desert planet and the shrewdness of an ecologist who saw what could be achieved not so much in spite of limitations imposed on life by the harsh characteristics of the desert but by manipulating them to the advantage of the inhabitants. In the true deserts of our own real world, where there is very little water or none at all, plants cannot grow, but there are large areas of that world where, although very dry conditions prevail, sufficient water exists to support plant life if the plant is prepared to adapt itself. In the course of evolutionary change, many plants have done so. Such plants have developed an appearance and characteristics quite different from those of dwellers in wetter places and have changed both themselves and the look of their landscape to such an extent that the extravagancies of science fiction cease to be unreal.

It is not only plants living in the semi-deserts of the hotter countries that suffer from drought. High up in mountain ranges the sun scorches down through the thin air and bakes the plants that grow there against the rocks. The high winds of those lonely altitudes also blow away moisture from the scanty soil. Even though it is frequently renewed by cloud or rain the intervals are all too brief when the plant has enough. Then, when the cold comes, the water freezes and might as well be in the moon for all the use the plants can make of it.

On the salt flats of the seacoast, the sea and land breezes blow unhindered across the vegetation and the sun beats down without shade of tree to mollify its effects. The plants of those places struggle to retain what water they have been able to extract from the salty wastes around them, knowing full well that, to replace the water which they lose, they must fight for every drop against the inhibiting salt, which limits absorption.

In a dry soil, one of the plant's chief aids in the struggle for water is an extensive root system. This may serve in two ways. If it is the upper layers of the soil only that are dried out and water may be found below, then a well developed root system can seek it out, no matter how far down it is. Generally, however, plants which grow in dry lands are not so fortunate and have to get their water in other ways. In areas of low rainfall the rain often comes in short sharp showers, separated by long intervals stretching into months. In these conditions, the plant which flourishes best is that which spreads its roots very widely and shallowly, almost on the surface, ready to gulp instantly the tiniest drop of water which comes its way. Some cacti help themselves still further by having downward pointed spines

Above: *A cultivated agave growing in Réunion, far from its native America. The agaves are of great use economically and are cultivated extensively for their fibre. The stumps of the leaves which have been cut from this specimen can be seen.*

Right: *An aloe named on the drawing* Aloe bowieana *after James Bowie, a Kew plant collector who made several journeys in South Africa in about 1820 and sent so many succulent plants to Kew that extra glasshouse space had to be provided.*

Aloe ferox, *a species with stout reddish teeth along its edges. Aloes are chiefly valued for their decorative foliage. The leaves in this species are very thick and long, gradually tapering from a wide base; they are held in a dense rosette. The flowers are orange, crowded into a conical spike. Aloes hybridise well and have been the subject of scientific work at Kew in recent years.*

When Sir William Hooker took over Kew he found two old Agaves. 'On one and the same day . . . in 1844,' he wrote, 'each was seen to produce a flowering stem. . . .' They grew at the same pace and 'at the very time it was found necessary to make an aperture in the glass roof . . . for the emission of one panicle of flowers a similar release was needed by the other!'

Right: Fine spikes of Agave americana, one of the larger agaves, making a stem up to twenty-five feet high. The rosette of leaves is large, the individual leathery grey-green leaves being three feet long. This species comes from Mexico but is naturalised along the coast of the Mediterranean.

Below: A charming portrait of a cactus by the most famous of all botanical artists, Georg Dionysus Ehret, whose works are now greatly prized. This illustration appeared in a collection of Plantae Selectae published at Augsburg by Dr C. J. Trew as part of a series in 1752. Ehret worked for a long time in Great Britain where his work was so appreciated that he was taken up by the fashionable world.

Far left: The Devil's Head Cactus from Brazil growing in the wild. This picture illustrates very well the attractiveness of these plants which has led to their great popularity and to the establishment of many societies of enthusiasts.

Left: Portrait of an aloe in the wild in its native South Africa. This shows why aloes are so attractive to the gardener and illustrates too the kind of dry and inhospitable terrain where they may be found.

which will collect the lightest dew or mist into droplets that fall off the points above the roots. Others have similar arrangements using different parts of the plant.

Having obtained the water, it is of vital importance that the plant does not lose it and lets it go only grudgingly as its life-processes require. Some plants endure a blistering soil temperature of 140 degrees Fahrenheit (60 degrees Centigrade) with air of a very low moisture content. To withstand such conditions considerable changes in plant structure are needed. Plants normally lose water through their leaves, so most of them dispense entirely with leaves or bear them for a short time only, in order to avoid the best part of this loss. Most of the cacti come into this category. They also turn almost all the cells of the stem into water-storage vessels, protecting them with a thick outer skin and reducing the cells devoted to the task of food production, usually performed mainly by the leaves, to a thin layer only.

These drastic measures produce an extraordinary change in the plant's appearance, making it quite unlike the normal herb with stem, branches and leaves. The stem of the prickly pears consists of a branching system of joints, but other plants either become round and ball-like or grow into a column, which may be quite tall. Anyone seeing the plants of dry lands for the first time may be excused for thinking their appearance bizarre, particularly as many of them are spiny. Their round and rod-like shapes have, of course, a distinct advantage over other possible forms, as they present less surface to the air and thus reduce water loss. They are, however, able to grow only slowly, because food production has had to take a back seat.

Plants which do not go as far as dispensing with leaves do, of course, present a larger surface from which they can lose moisture to the dry air and must adjust their arrangements

.Tab. XXXI.

This magnificent plant is one of those included in the collection of Plantae Selectae *by C. J. Trew, the illustrations for which were drawn by G. D. Ehret. This particular picture appeared in the section published in 1754. It bears the name* Cereus gracilis *but may be the species now known as* Selenicereus grandiflorus, *the 'Queen of the Night', a native of Jamaica. It represents very well the night-flowering cacti whose very large white flowers glow like moons in the tropic dusk. The plant itself is quite slender, the stem being ribbed, and produces aerial roots, which Ehret has shown clearly in his picture. The large juicy fruit borne by these plants is covered with spines which may be shed. Cacti appear so heavily armoured that it requires an effort of the imagination to envisage that, inside their tough outer covering, they grow at all, but, although not among the most rapid growers, these climbing cacti do very well, making three feet or more a year of new growth.*

This particular cactus is an inhabitant of a warm West Indian island. Practically all cacti live in such locations, though there are a few that have adapted themselves to the cold and live up at great heights in the Andes, some species even being covered with snow in the winter!

On 12 March 1844, the Royal Botanic Gardens received from Mr Frederick Staines of San Luis Potosi in Mexico what was then a very large Echinocactus (a kind of cactus cylindrical or globular in shape) which weighed 235 lbs and excited much interest. In February 1845, however, Mr Staines sent a much larger one weighing 713 lbs, but even this monster was in turn surpassed by a giant weighing a ton which was received on 10 July 1846. Unfortunately, although this specimen arrived in reasonably good condition apart from two or three small bruises, these bruises became infected and began to rot, and it was not long before the huge plant perished in a mass of unpleasant-smelling corruption!

Below: Aloe mitriformis, *a native of Cape Province. This species has red flowers.*
Opposite: Agaves in flower at a Royal Horticultural Society show in Victorian times. Note on the right the 'ghost' of a chair captured by the time-exposure; someone had obviously forgotten to move it, and it was snatched away after the photographer had started – but not before the film had caught it!

accordingly. Their leaves are provided with a very thick skin, often furnished with white hairs or coated with wax, and, as with the stem of the leafless forms, are frequently ball-like or of a rod shape. Quite often they are pressed closely to the stem, which in some cases disappears altogether, so that the plant again becomes more or less round in shape. Another form which is very common is the rosette, which may close up to form a ball if the heat becomes greater than the plant wishes to tolerate.

The change in the shape of the individual plants greatly affects the appearance of the landscape in the places where they grow. The trees and grass of the wetter lands provide a green soft-textured cover which conceals the harshness of the underlying soil and rocks. In the dry lands, however, this cover is absent, and the basic scene stands out stark and rugged, unrelieved by anything to soften it, the vegetation being sparsely scattered, each plant snatching a living where it can. The plants that live out their unassuming lives in these inhospitable places are so grotesque in shape that they add to the savagery and wildness of the scene rather than relieve it.

Some of the plants that grow in the very hottest places and have reduced themselves to a single body have developed an ingenious way of modifying the extreme heat of the sun as it beats down on them hour after hour like the hot glow from a furnace. A kind of window is formed in the flat top of the plant, the skin containing crystals which impede the passage and reduce the power of the sunlight. No more is allowed to pass through than is needed for food production deep within the plant body.

As well as the plants which have taken these extreme measures to combat the harshness of the environment there are others that are usually classed with them but have not found it necessary to change to the same degree, since they do not have to face quite such adverse conditions. In these plants adaptation for storage is mostly confined to the stem, which is swollen or bulbous above ground, the leaves being retained and differing somewhat less from normal than in the case of the extreme

Above: Portrait of Francis Masson. When Sir Joseph Banks returned in 1772 from his voyage with Captain Cook he impressed George III so much with his account of the world's vegetation that the King was induced to send a plant collector (the first official Kew plant collector) with Cook on his second voyage. The Kew gardener chosen was Francis Masson, who sent back a large number of plants from South Africa including many succulents.

forms. It is not customary to class as succulents plants which have bulbs or tubers below ground, like the ordinary garden bulbs, although many of these adopt their mode of growth so that they can more easily withstand periods of dryness.

The mass of water-storage cells which the plants we have been considering contain makes them thick and fleshy, and the term 'succulent', which means just this, has come into use to describe them. The phrase 'Cacti and Succulents' is often used to refer to such plants, but this is like saying 'Men and People' – the second word includes the first. Cacti are not separate from succulents, they are merely the largest family included in that term.

The cacti are natives of the western hemisphere and are the dominant vegetation of the driest parts. Many of them are armed with spines which are a necessary protection, as, being fleshy they would, without this defence, present a tempting morsel to any hungry predator. They vary greatly in size and appearance, some being small and button-like, while others make tall branched columns like trees, which have a woody skeleton and can reach fifty feet or more in height. Many cacti have large, attractive and brightly coloured flowers: some are climbers and, strangely enough, some are found where they might be least expected, in the tropical rain-forests. Here they live as epiphytes in situations which are, in spite of the rain, almost as dry as those of their semi-desert relatives. They draw no water from their host, on which they are merely perched; in similar situations, orchids find it necessary to make aerial roots specially adapted to extract moisture from the air. Cacti, which do not also develop this facility, must adopt their usual means to survive.

A number of cacti are night flowering, taking advantage of the pollinators about in the coolness of that time. The flowers of these kinds are generally white, being more easily seen in the dim light.

Although cacti are known in the temperate zone mainly as ornamental plants, they are of great economic importance in Mexico, the Caribbean and Central and South America, where they are cultivated for food. Some kinds are also used widely for planting as fences around houses, forming an impenetrable boundary.

Another group of succulent plants found in the western hemisphere is sometimes confused with the cacti. The agaves resemble cacti, but storage is in the leaves, particularly the bases, rather than the stems. The leaves form a thick fleshy rosette from which springs a long spike of yellowish or greenish flowers. Some kinds, particularly the larger ones, take many years to bloom, and agaves have for this reason been called 'Century Plants', it being supposed that they do not flower until they are a hundred years old. Some, in fact, flower annually, others every few years, but many do flower only once and then die – not, however, before developing in most cases basal suckers which will become new plants. Although some agaves are comparatively small, there are others which are very large plants. One kind has leaves eight feet long and sends up a flower stalk as thick as a man's body thirty feet high. The flower

Right: Euphorbia is such a large and diverse genus that it is not possible to select a species and say that it is typical. The plant shown in this illustration has therefore been selected at random as a representative of the other species (more than a thousand) comprised in the genus. One of the most striking plants in it is E. pulcherrima, the familiar Poinsettia, used so much as a decorative plant or for cut flowers. Another free-flowering species useful for decoration is E. fulgens, a leafy shrub with slender branches bearing conspicuous scarlet flowers in small clusters along the branches. Most of the succulent Euphorbias are natives of Africa, and a characteristic of the genus is the milky latex which exudes when they are damaged. This is often poisonous, though some kinds are used by local inhabitants as medicine. The succulent types, a temptation to the thirsty animal, are generally well armed with spines.
Opposite: A leafy aloe well armed with defensive spines on its long slender tapering leaves, a very necessary protection.

Above: A curious Euphorbia of Cape Province photographed in the wild. The appearance of this species is a considerable contrast to that of the other Euphorbia *opposite and illustrates the diversity of the genus. The name* Euphorbia *is of some interest, as it was given by the Greek Dioscorides and is said by Pliny to have been chosen to honour Euphorbus, physician to Juba, King of Mauritania.*

stalk of another kind has been known to reach forty-two feet.

Agaves are important economically as a source of fibre for making cordage and are cultivated extensively for this purpose. They contribute greatly to the gaiety of Mexican life by providing the material for fermented beverages, and great plantations are maintained for this purpose. They serve as hedgerows and are of help in the control of erosion.

The rest of the succulents, but not all, are mainly found in Africa. There is, indeed, in that continent a counterpart to the cacti, as the large genus of euphorbias contains a number of members which are cactus-like, although their flowers are dissimilar and they have a milky juice not found in cacti. The agaves also have a counterpart widespread in Africa – the aloes. Indeed, the resemblance is so close that the agave is called the 'American Aloe'.

Included in one family found in Africa are some strange plants which grow among stones and resemble them so much that when they are not flowering they are very difficult to see. These have reduced themselves so far that they are a single small body only. Many of them have a split which shows that they have developed from a plant with two leaves, this vestige being all that is left to indicate the fact. When these small plants flower, they present a remarkable appearance, the flowers being larger than the plant which bears them!

Another large family of succulents, scattered more widely than most of the others, includes the stonecrops and the houseleeks, familiar in Great Britain on rock gardens and walls. The common British weed, the groundsel, has a number of succulent relatives which those acquainted with it as no more than an insignificant nuisance may find surprising. The ubiquitous garden geranium, more properly called a *Pelargonium*, itself somewhat fleshy, represents a genus with a number of succulent members.

Succulent plants affect different people in different ways. Many people find their fantastic shapes absorbing, and few can dislike their bright and showy flowers. They also have a considerable following among growers of house-plants because of the ease with which many of them can be cultivated. On the other hand, their spiny nature makes them difficult to handle when they become a nuisance, as the prickly pear did in Australia, and there are those who find them grotesque and repulsive rather than attractive. Whatever one feels about them, it is impossible to deny that they are plants of great character, thoroughly adapted to their own world.

Before Adam

'Ancestral images,
Ere that unfallen Eden had its day
Of yet undimmed forest and flower. . . .'
A.E.

The media have made most of us familiar with the term 'living fossil', but what precisely does it mean? A thing cannot be both a 'fossil' – an impression preserved in the rocks of something that used to be living – which is dead, and 'living' at the same time. The phrase is, of course, a kind of convenient shorthand to denote something which exists as a living organism at present but which is also known, from the evidence of the rocks, to have been in existence in very much the same form in the remote geological past.

Forms do not persist virtually unchanged for hundreds of millions of years if they are not well adapted to their environment, and the plant, animal or insect which merits the status of 'living fossil' receives, in effect, the supreme evolutionary accolade because it has been classed in the select band of organisms which have had the highest success in the battle for survival. There are many more plants in this category than the few of which we are aware, as the evidence of the rocks is not only fragmentary and imperfect but, over a very wide range, absent altogether.

One we do know about, and of which we have had knowledge for some time, is the Maidenhair Tree; this has the curious botanical name of *Ginkgo biloba*, which was given to it by the great botanist Linnaeus in 1771. When mature the Maidenhair Tree is a fine upright tree of stiffish spiky growth with a rough grey trunk which one writer has compared to the hide of an elephant. The leaves are fanshaped, the veins being forked, and resemble the leaves of the Maidenhair Fern, from which it takes its name. They are often two-lobed – hence the specific name *biloba* – and are borne either scattered on long shoots or crowded together at the top of short stubby shoots. The leaves turn an attractive yellow before they are shed in the autumn.

The flowers, borne in May on the shorter twigs, are quite small. The male flowers are yellowish green catkins which are not particularly difficult to see, but the female flowers are liable to escape observation. They are normally borne on separate plants, but branches of a tree of one sex will grow if grafted on a tree of the other. The female flower consists of a stalk with two ovules surrounded at the base with a collar. As the ovules are not enclosed the seeds, when they develop from them after fertilisation, are not in a pod or capsule; thus the Maidenhair Tree is a 'naked seeded' plant – known botanically as a gymnosperm. It is one of the most primitive plants in this division and is near, in an evolutionary sense, to the cycads (a primitive cone-bearing group of plants) and the ferns.

The Maidenhair Tree, or its very near relatives, is found in fossil form in geological deposits which can be dated as far back as Permian times, which was the last stage of the Palaeozoic era,

some 260 million years ago. It was once very widespread in the north temperate zone. Although it has survived that incredibly long period, it has gradually been losing ground recently, and only one small rather doubtfully wild group is supposed to exist in nature at the present time – in China. It found favour, however, with both the Chinese and the Japanese as an ornamental tree for temple courtyards, and many specimens have been preserved in this way.

The Maidenhair Tree first came to the notice of the western world when it was discovered in 1690 by Dr Engelbert Kaempfer, a surgeon in the employ of the Dutch East India Company. He wrote an account of it in a book he published in 1712. A few years afterwards, between 1727 and 1737, living plants arrived in Holland, and one of these survives in the Utrecht Botanic Garden to this day. A specimen was planted at Kew in 1762, not long after the botanic garden was founded. This is now a fine tree and one of the best known sights of Kew. The name *Ginkgo* was taken by Linnaeus from Kaempfer, but there is no record of its origin beyond this. The word is unknown in Japan and China except as a western botanical name. Modern opinion is that *Ginkgo* is a corruption or error of transcription and has no meaning. By the rules of botanical nomenclature, however, the Maidenhair Tree is saddled with this rather bizarre cognomen!

Since its introduction to the west the Maidenhair Tree has become widely grown for its ornamental qualities a well as its interest as a 'living fossil' and is often used as a street tree. Authorities recommend, however, that the male tree only

Above: A young Maidenhair Tree, Ginkgo biloba, *growing, appropriately enough, on the site of the Temple of the Sun, one of Sir William Chambers' classical temples, which marked the centre of the original nine-acre botanic garden. The temple, probably the most elegant of Sir William Chambers' small classical works at Kew, was smashed to pieces by the fall in 1916 of a Cedar of Lebanon.*

Opposite: The best-known tree in Kew Gardens. This fine mature Maidenhair Tree was planted in 1762 just after the botanic garden was founded. A male tree, it at one time bore a female branch which had been grafted on it. This branch has not survived, the story being that it was pruned off by an over-enthusiastic gardener! It is more likely that it died.

should be used: the seed is covered with a fleshy coating which has an offensive smell when it rots and can make pavements foul, so the female tree which bears the fruit should be avoided. This fleshy covering is nauseous to eat, though the 'nut' within it is commonly eaten in the Far East.

In fossils examined by botanists in the early 1940s were some which had been classed with the giant coastal redwoods of California but which were felt on re-examination to be separate. They were accordingly, in 1941, put in a new genus called *Metasequoia*. In 1945 three large trees of what appeared to be an unknown conifer were discovered in China, in north-eastern Szechuan, very close to the Hupeh border. When specimens from this tree were examined by botanists they were astounded to find that it so closely resembled their new genus that it undoubtedly had to be regarded as a member of it – a new 'living fossil' had been found!

The new species is called the Dawn Redwood. It is a little younger than the Maidenhair Tree as it originated in the age of the dinosaurs – the Mezozoic age. Like the Maidenhair Tree, it was formerly very widely spread but became extinct in Europe and North America about fifteen million years ago, lingering on a little longer in Japan. By the time it was discovered, it had dwindled in numbers in its last home, China, so far that it was on the verge of extinction. A search in the area where the original trees were found revealed about a thousand more, mostly in the Shui-sa-pa valley in the province of Hupeh. The valley had been named after the tree, the Chinese name for it being *Shui-sa*, which means water spruce. The tree is fond of water and seems to grow best beside streams or in wet soil. The region in which it grows is subject to ice and snow in the winter and it has not been found at elevations above four thousand feet, appearing to prefer a mild winter temperature. It was growing alongside chestnut, sweet gum, oak and birch.

Seed imported into the USA in 1948 and passed on to other countries germinated readily, and by now the tree is widely distributed. Although some specimens have already attained a good size it is not yet known how big the tree will grow in western countries. The tallest tree seen in the wild was 115 feet high and $7\frac{1}{2}$ feet in diameter. In suitable moist and mild conditions there seems no reason to believe that the Dawn Redwood will not attain the same stature in the west. Although it sheds its leaves in the winter, all summer it is covered with a most attractive soft feathery green foliage which, for those who know it, is reminiscent of the Swamp or Bald Cypress. In

autumn the leaves assume an even more attractive pinkish-brown tint before they are shed.

It has often been stated that the Maidenhair Tree was regarded as sacred by the Chinese and that it was for this reason preserved within temple precincts. In the modern standard reference work, Willis's *Dictionary of Flowering Plants and Ferns*, which was revised in 1973 by Mr. H. K. Airy Shaw of Kew, the statement is, however, made that 'the tree is often but erroneously regarded as sacred'. Ann Bridge described in her novel *Peking Picnic* a tree that she had actually seen, the treatment of which confirmed the former view. 'In the largest court of all [of the monastery]', she said, 'stands a *Ginkgo* tree of unknown age and immense size . . . which a few centuries back was canonised as a saint and also elevated to the peerage with title corresponding to that of marquess. At the foot of its great silvery-yellowish trunk stands a little altar where the pious may burn joss sticks in its honour; close by a carved tablet bears its parent of nobility . . . .' In correspondence about this passage she added 'in the month of September, 1926 I passed through Tan Chueh Su, and the ground in the great courtyard was entirely covered with the little apple-shaped fruits of the *Ginkgo*, on long stalks like cherries, in bunches of two to five'.

It is claimed too that the Dawn Redwood is sacred. Indeed, an illustration of it that appeared at the time it was discovered said: 'This is a sacred tree as indicated by the small Todee temple in front of the tree. Todee meaning God of the Land.' Whatever the truth is about the religious significance of these two 'living fossils', the tremendous length of their existence virtually unchanged will always render them objects of interest to be preserved and venerated.

Above left: *The foliage of the Maidenhair Tree, from which the primitive nature of the leaves – the veins radiate out like a fan from the base – and their resemblance in shape to those of the Maidenhair Fern can clearly be seen.*

Above: *The foliage of the Dawn Redwood,* Metasequoia glyptostroboides, *is a most attractive feature of the tree, being a soft feathery green in*

summer and changing to a beautiful pinkish brown in the autumn before it is shed.

Opposite: *The Dawn Redwood in Kew Gardens. Larger trees exist elsewhere, but no one knows how large the* Metasequoia *will grow in the British Isles, since the oldest there has been growing only since the late 1940s, when it was discovered.*

Water, Water Everywhere

*'Where the pool
Eddies away, are tangled mass on mass
The water-weeds, that net the fishes cool,
And scarce allow the narrow stream to pass.'*
Robert Bridges

Sir Joseph Paxton, the first man to succeed in cultivating the Giant Water Lily of South America, the Victoria amazonica, *in Europe. Kew had raised plants but lost them. When a second batch was raised, Sir William Hooker asked Sir Joseph Paxton to try one. He took it off to Chatsworth, where he was gardener to the Duke of Devonshire, and built a special glasshouse for it. His letters to the Duke of Devonshire, in Ireland at the time, show mounting excitement as the day approached when the first flower opened.*

When you come to think of it, all plants are in a way aquatic, because even those which grow in the driest places on land are dependent upon an uninterrupted supply of water for survival. If they cannot get it, they eventually die. There are a few which live without roots, but they depend on the moisture in the air. Water is the major constituent of living tissues, and there is little doubt that, whatever way they originated, the first living things lived wholly in the water. This is the sense in which the term 'aquatic' is usually taken, and any account of such plants must begin with the point that their mode of living was the first that was ever known on this planet.

Aquatic plants still include many simple minute living things not far removed from the original organisms, as a glance through a microscope at a slide of pond scum will show, but they also include many more complex ones, up to and including the flowering plants. One group with which most of us are very familiar from our seaside holidays is the seaweeds. Their name indicates how widespread they are – the weeds of the sea! In contrast with the little plants of the pond scum, some of the seaweeds are giants, growing to a length of more than a hundred feet. Some relatives of the seaweeds, which are algae, grow in fresh water. Other groups low in the evolutionary scale which have members adapted to an aquatic existence are the mosses and liverworts and the ferns and their allies. The larger plants of fresh water are, however, all flowering plants.

It may seem fantastic, in an organism which depends, as plants do, upon sunlight and air for making its food, that some should have gone so far against their natural inclinations as to have adapted themselves to live wholly submerged, where the light is dim and air scarce, but such is the case! At the other end of the scale are those which merely root in the water but whose leaves and stems are held up in the air. These include those ubiquitous plants the reeds and rushes. Another group, among which are the water ferns, do not root on the bottom but float free on the surface. A fourth group, that contains the water lilies, the most beautiful of the aquatic plants, is rooted on the bottom but has leaves which float on the surface.

One of the difficulties with which aquatic plants have to contend is the lack of air for those parts which are below the surface of the water. This difficulty they have overcome by evolving special tissue, spongier than normal, through which air is moved from the upper parts down to those under the water. Most aquatic plants prefer quiet water, but a few have adapted themselves to live in rapid currents. The chief factor in the well-being of the majority, however, is the same as in land plants, the fertility of the bottom soil. If this is lacking in essential plant foods, water plants will not flourish, any more

Opposite top: Victoria cruziana *at Kew in the Tropical Water Lily House. The flower buds can be seen just to the left of the label, the open flowers in the photograph being those of other species of water-lily growing in the tank.* V. cruziana *is a close relative of* V. amazonica *but slightly smaller.*
Opposite: The Sacred Lotus growing wild in Kenya. The flowers of this long-venerated plant are pure white, tinged pink at the base of the outer petals. They open on four successive nights.

***Below:** Hydrocleys nymphoides, a tropical South American plant with large yellow flowers somewhat resembling the water-lily in habit but less attractive.*

than land plants do on poor soils. Where aquatic plants do prosper, they can be very vigorous and invasive. There are many large wet areas in the world where water and marsh plants are the dominant vegetation. The distinction between water and marsh plants is blurred, as many aquatic plants are quite able to grow in wet soil and need not actually be in the water, although their characteristics may differ quite markedly between the two habitats. The Arrowhead, for example, develops its characteristic leaves, from which it gets its name, only as a marsh plant. When growing as a submerged plant its leaves remain ribbonlike.

Individual species often cover large areas of water entirely. Duckweeds form a green sheet over many ponds and pondweeds grow thickly in many lakes. Water plants are, indeed, often a nuisance in choking narrow channels which it is essential to keep open for irrigation or drainage. Their vigour has often been displayed when, accidentally or by intent, one has been taken to a new region or country. In the last century the Canadian Waterweed was inadvertently introduced into Europe and within a remarkably short time became a serious

Right: Water lilies in flower in the Tropical Water Lily House at Kew Gardens.
Below: Victoria amazonica at Kew Gardens. The difficulties experienced at first in growing this plant in Great Britain arose because it was not realised that the temperature of the water in which the plant grows must not fall lower than 80°F (85°F when young). Light was also a problem. The soft light of Great Britain is a poor substitute for the tropical glare to which the plant is accustomed in its natural habitat.
Bottom: The flower of Victoria amazonica, *then called* V. regia, *as drawn by W. H. Fitch to illustrate* Victoria regia, or Illustrations of the Royal Water Lily *by Sir W. J. Hooker, published in 1851.*

pest in inland waters. The free-floating plants are great culprits in this respect, the Water Hyacinth of South America being one of the worst and most widespread of the water-weeds. The White Nile is one of the rivers that has been greatly affected by the growth of vegetation. Masses of plants from the papyrus-reed swamps in the upper reaches have sometimes broken away and completely blocked the channel, and lower down it used to be completely closed for long reaches by the 'sudd', similar masses of plant material from the extensive Sudd marshes.

Water plants function as basic food producers for their habitat. They provide food for fish, insects, animals, wildfowl and human beings. (Most of us are acquainted with watercress, a common salad plant). In the process of photosynthesis, they perform the essential task of oxygenating the water so that it becomes habitable for fish and other aquatic living organisms. The less vigorous aquatic plants are grown in aquaria for this purpose. The submerged plants also provide cover for the denizens of the water which need it, particularly the young. Those plants which form growth above the water provide safe and hospitable habitats for both birds and mammals.

Some of the water plants are grown for ornament in suitable habitats specially constructed for them in gardens. Of the ornamental water plants, by far the most attractive is the water lily family, which throws up the most beautiful many-petalled showy flowers in shades of white, red, yellow and blue, each several inches across. The water-lilies are, in the main, natives of the northern hemisphere, where they are very widespread, but there are some tropical kinds. These include the remarkable Giant Water Lily, the *Victoria amazonica*. This plant grows in the backwaters of the Amazon, sometimes in great profusion, covering the water for considerable distances. Those who are acquainted with the smaller water lilies only will find this plant unbelievably large. Its leaves may reach nearly seven feet in diameter and its flowers are up to eighteen inches across. It was first described by botanists in 1837, and when seeds received at Kew in the 1840s were germinated they could not at first be got to grow. That remarkable man, Joseph Paxton, designer and railway tycoon as well as gardener to the Duke of Devonshire at Chatsworth, was given a plant by Kew and in 1848 succeeded in getting it to flower. He took the cellular structure of the underside of the leaf as a model for the successful design of the Crystal Palace which he submitted to the Fine Arts Commis-

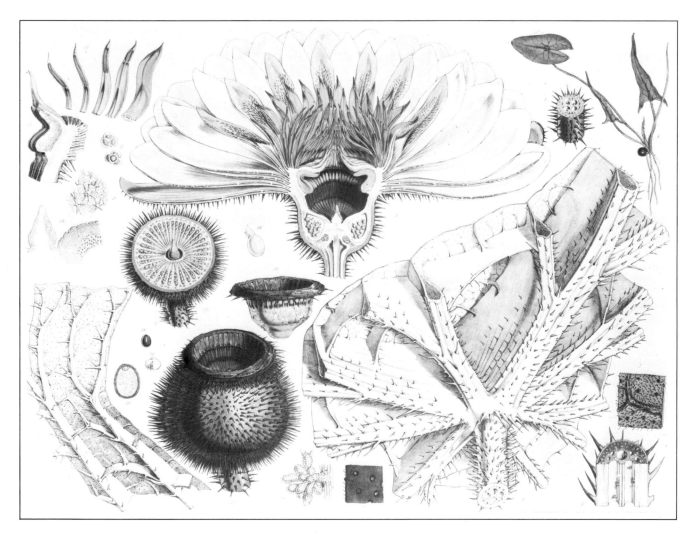

Top: *Parts of the* Victoria amazonica *drawn by W. H. Fitch for Sir W. J. Hooker's* Victoria regia.
Above: *Drawing by William Sharp of the underside of a leaf of* Victoria amazonica *showing detail of the structure. This appeared in a publication entitled* Victoria regia or the Giant Water Lily of America *by J. F. Allen, published in Boston, USA, in 1854. The drawing shows the ribs or veins which project underneath, dividing the surface into a number of pockets which give the leaf great buoyancy. Paxton is said to have allowed his small daughter to stand on a leaf and found that it supported her. The leaves will, indeed, take the weight of a small child, providing it stands on a flat board which distributes the weight evenly over the whole leaf.*

sion, taking a leaf along with him to show them. Paxton having pointed the way, the Giant Water Lily was soon being grown and flowering at Kew and became immediately one of the sights of the Gardens, which it has remained ever since. In nature it is a perennial, but it is difficult to keep through the gloomy English winter and is grown at Kew as an annual. The seed, the size of a pea, is sown in January; by August its leaves are five to six feet across and it completely fills the large tank in which it is grown.

Another lily, as remarkable in its way as the Giant Water Lily, is the Sacred Lotus of India and China. This was first used as a symbol in ancient Egypt and afterwards acquired a religious significance for all Buddhists and Hindus: in Tibet it is the common vehicle for amulets and charms. It is part of the famous prayer *Om mani padme hum*, which can be translated as 'Hail to the Jewel in the Lotus' and is inscribed everywhere in Tibet and recited endlessly to the turning of the prayer wheel. The plant has more humdrum uses for food and medicine. It grows along the edges of lakes, producing large pink flowers which are held at a height of one to two and a half feet above the water and, later, distinctive 'pepper pot' seedpods. The seed has remarkable powers of survival, having germinated after being buried by a chance of nature in a layer known to have been undisturbed for four hundred years.

Although they do not, in the main, have to struggle for existence against great adversity, like the plants of arid places, aquatic plants also adapt themselves to extreme conditions, in their case too much water rather than too little, and thus have an interest beyond the ordinary. Life on earth began with organisms that lived in water. It is fitting that this book, coming full circle, should end with a chapter on plants which still live in such a habitat and fitting also that some of them, the water-lilies, should be among the most beautiful of all plants.

Index

Picture Credits

The pictures in this book are Crown Copyright and have been reproduced with permission of the Controller of Her Majesty's Stationery Office and of the Director, Royal Botanic Gardens, Kew, with the following exceptions: The Courtauld Institute of Art p12 bottom left; G C K Dunsterville p65 and p69 bottom left; Dr Richard A Howard p108 bottom left; Mrs D Jeffes p112 bottom right; David Warner p26 right, p31 top and bottom,
p52 top left and top right, p53 right, p56 top, p57 top, p71, p84, p86 right, p118, p120 left and right, p121, p123 top left, p124 top and middle